T0277119

Cambridge Elements ≡

Elements in Phonology
edited by
Robert Kennedy
University of California, Santa Barbara
Patrycja Strycharczuk
University of Manchester

COMPLEXITY
IN THE PHONOLOGY
OF TONE

Lian-Hee Wee
Hong Kong Baptist University
Mingxing Li
Hong Kong Baptist University

CAMBRIDGE
UNIVERSITY PRESS

Shaftesbury Road, Cambridge CB2 8EA, United Kingdom

One Liberty Plaza, 20th Floor, New York, NY 10006, USA

477 Williamstown Road, Port Melbourne, VIC 3207, Australia

314–321, 3rd Floor, Plot 3, Splendor Forum, Jasola District Centre,
New Delhi – 110025, India

103 Penang Road, #05–06/07, Visioncrest Commercial, Singapore 238467

Cambridge University Press is part of Cambridge University Press & Assessment,
a department of the University of Cambridge.

We share the University's mission to contribute to society through the pursuit of
education, learning and research at the highest international levels of excellence.

www.cambridge.org
Information on this title: www.cambridge.org/9781009078061

DOI: 10.1017/9781009086707

First published 2023

A catalogue record for this publication is available from the British Library.

ISBN 978-1-009-07806-1 Paperback
ISSN 2633-9064 (online)
ISSN 2633-9056 (print)

Additional resources for this publication at www.cambridge.org/wee-li

Complexity in the Phonology of Tone

Elements in Phonology

DOI: 10.1017/9781009086707
First published online: October 2023

Lian-Hee Wee
Hong Kong Baptist University

Mingxing Li
Hong Kong Baptist University

Author for correspondence: Lian-Hee Wee, lianhee@hkbu.edu.hk

Abstract: The complexity of tone can only be appreciated through phonological patterning that unveils structures beyond differences in pitch heights and contour profiles. Following an introduction on tone's ability to express lexical and grammatical contrasts, Section 2 explains that phonetically, fundamental frequency profiles make the best descriptors. From these descriptions, Section 3 explains how, through postulations of subatomic entities that comprise tones, a language's tone inventory can be quite symmetrical. In looking at tone's independence from the syllable and segments, Section 4 establishes tone as an autosegment. Sections 5, 6, and 7 go on to discuss a myriad of complexities where tones interact with one another and with other phonological entities. Here, the authors offer a suggestion on how some of these interactions can be captured within the same analytical umbrella. Section 8 then peeks into tone's phonological properties through music and poetry.

This Element also has a video abstract: www.cambridge.org/complexity_abstract

Keywords: tone, sandhi, tonology, phonology, phonetics

ISBNs: 9781009078061 (PB), 9781009086707 (OC)
ISSNs: 2633-9064 (online), 2633-9056 (print)

Contents

1 Complexities of Tone

In the theoretical study of linguistics, tone was not given much attention until rather late in modern times. The IPA chart, for example, included tone and pitch marks under 'additional notes' for the first time only in 1932. Then, as is still the case now, tones were described in terms of melodic profiles such as high, low, rising, falling, and so on. At the simplest level of understanding, these different melodic profiles corresponded to contrasts in meanings, exemplified in Tables 1 and 2.

In some languages, such as Wàpá and Igala, the melody applies across syllables (see Tables 3 and 4).

While such descriptions are phonetically faithful, the phonological complexities that are presented by tones can only be apprehended through a much more sophisticated model. This Element shall endeavour to demonstrate these complexities.

Humanity had, of course, been aware of pitch modulations in spoken languages before the twentieth century. With regard to ancient scholarship, the earliest mentions were Indian, Greek, and Chinese. In India, Pāṇini's *Aṣṭādhyāyī* (circa fourth century BCE) expounded on the Vedic accents *udātta* 'raised, high pitch', *anudātta* 'not raised, low pitch', and *svarita* 'sounded, falling pitch'. In classical Greek, the acute, grave, macron, and circumflex accent marks presumably indicated melodic shapes, as they relate to such musical terms as *tonos* 'tone, lit. to stretch (the strings of musical instruments)', *okseia* 'sharp, high', and *bareia* 'low'. From a facsimile of the thirteenth-century copy of the Periplus of Pseudo-Scylax, dating back to the mid-fourth century BCE, we know that Dionysus Thrax (second–first century BCE) described these accents in musical terms. However, given that classical Greek and Sanskrit are not known to involve tone contrasts at the level of words, it remains uncertain whether these are diacritics for musical chanting. The Romans probably inherited the Greek symbols in the form of the neume, a type of diacritic mark found in Latin liturgical texts to denote proper intoning.

Modern interpretations of historical texts suggest that the earliest known Chinese scholarship that makes references to linguistic tone comes from the fifth century CE. Also, traditional Chinese scholarship would include the field of *xiaoxue* 'small learning'; this covers *wenzixue* 'orthographic studies', which deals with Chinese characters, *shengyunxue* 'phonology', and *xunguxue* 'exegesis', all of which are philological in nature and in the service of apprehending archaic documents.

Yip (2002: 1) suggests that by some estimates, 60–70 per cent of the world's languages may be tonal. For Yip, a tone language is one in which 'the pitch of a word can change the meaning of the word'. The examples in Tables 1–4, of Thai, Yoruba, Wàpá, and Igala, have illustrated this lexical function of tone. In addition,

Table 1 Tones in Thai (Hudak 2009)

Tone	[na]	[khaa]	[mai]
High	'mother's younger sibling'	'to do business in'	'wood'
Mid	'paddy field'	'to be lodged in'	'mile'
Low	a nickname	a kind of aromatic root	'new'
Falling	'face'	'servant'	'no/not'
Rising	'thick'	'leg'	'silk'

Table 2 Tones in Yoruba
(Awobuluyi 1978: 148; Akinlabi and Liberman 2000: 33; Peng 2013: 346)

Tone	[ra]	[bu]	[bɔ]
High	'to disappear'	'to insult'	'to drop'
Mid	'to rob'	'to mildew'	'to worship'
Low	'to buy'	'to break off'	'to come'

Table 3 Tones in Wàpã
(Welmers 1973: 116)

ak	wi	
Mid	High	'knife'
Mid	Mid	'millstone'
Mid	Low	'chicken'
Low	Low	'gourd'

Table 4 Tones in Igala (Welmers 1973: 116)

a	wo	
High	High	'guinea fowl'
High	Mid	'an increase'
High	Low	'hole (in a tree)'
Low	High	'a slap'
Low	Mid	'a comb'
Low	Low	'star'

Table 5 Verb conjugation by tone in Iau (Bateman 1990: 35–6; Hyman and Leben 2020)

Verb	Gloss	Inflectional meaning
bá	'came'	Totality of actional punctual
bā	'has come'	Resultative durative
bá″	'might come'	Totality of action incompletive
bǎ	'came to get'	Resultative punctual
bâ	'came to endpoint'	Telic punctual
bá̄	'still not at endpoint'	Telic incompletive
bā̄	'come (process)'	Totality of action durative
bâ⁻	'sticking, attached to'	Telic durative

Table 6 Tones for case in Somali (from Yip 2002: 140, see also Hyman 1981, Banti 1988)

Nominative	Vocative	Genitive	Absolutive	
rag	-	rág	rág	'males'
orgi	órgi	orgí	órgi	'billy goat'
hooyooyin	hóoyooyin	hooyooyín	hooyoóyin	'mothers'
xaas	-	xaás	xáas	'family'

there are languages where differences in tone can signal grammatical function. An excellent example comes from Iau, a Lakes Plain language from West Papua, Indonesia (Bateman 1990: 35–6, cited in Hyman and Leben 2020), where tone signals verbal inflection (Table 5).

In Somali, tone signals differences in grammatical case.

In Table 6, the vowels carrying the accent mark (e.g., á, ó, í) are articulated with a high tone. As can be seen, words in the nominative case do not carry any marking (i.e., they are unmarked) for high melodies. With vocatives, the initial vowel would get a high melody, with genitives the final vowel and with absolutives the penultimate vowel. Tones can also indicate grammatical person. In Chimwiini, this is done by the position of the high tone, for example *jile: ṇamá* 'you sg. ate meat' contrasts with *jile: ṇáma* 's/he ate meat' (Kisseberth and Abasheikh 2011). For a succinct and comprehensive treatment of grammatical tone, see Hyman and Leben (2020).

Other than signalling lexical contrasts and grammatical markings, tone also appears to signal prosodic differences. In languages where prosody is described in terms of stress, the main acoustic correlate of stress is often fundamental frequency (F0). Thus, in English *uni<u>ver</u>sity*, the stressed syllable -*ver*- is normally articulated with a higher F0 than the other syllables. In perception experiments, syllables with higher F0 are more likely to be perceived as stressed than other parameters such as duration or intensity (Bolinger 1958, Fry 1958, Beckman 1986). In fact, Goldsmith (1978) suggested that stress and intonation may be treated with tone features (see also Gussenhoven 2004: 49–70). Depending on one's theoretical assumptions, languages like Japanese use placement of the high tone to distinguish meaning, which may seem an uncanny resemblance to stress placement in English (consider *reFUSE* 'to decline' with *REfuse* 'trash'). Perhaps for this reason, Japanese has often been described as pitch accented (McCawley 1978 may be the first to offer a theoretical treatment; de Lacy 2002 points out that pitch accents in many languages interact with stress).

In Table 7, the L and H stand for High and Low respectively. In Japanese, L is not part of the equation – any syllable not given H is L by default. Except for the initial syllable, all syllables preceding H would also be articulated as H. Thus, in the example in Table 7, H is assigned to the first syllable in *háshi-ga* 'chopstick', to the second in *hashí-ga* 'bridge', and the third in *hashí-gá* 'edge'. *Ga* is a nominative case marker. The properties of the Japanese-type pitch-accent system are also seen in languages that have not been conventionally recognized as tonal languages, such as Hong Kong English. There is some evidence that syllables in Hong Kong English are lexically specified for tones, similar to Japanese (Wee 2016a). This property may have been employed as a literary device in Hong Kong's English poetry (Wee 2016b).

In addition to all these, one must be aware that tones are not stable. The same syllable-morpheme may have a different tone depending on context (Shih 1986, Chen 2000, Zhang 2014, Wee 2019, among others). For example, in Hainanese, low-tone syllables become high when followed by another syllable (of any tone). In the same context, syllables with a falling tone become low (see Table 8).

Tone instability comes in many forms, and should be treated differently. In cases where tones alternate in collocation with others, it is often called tone

Table 7 Japanese pitch accent

Word	Melodic profile	Gloss
háshi-ga	H-L-L	'chopsticks'
hashí-ga	L-H-L	'bridge'
hashí-gá	L-H-H	'edge'

Table 8 Tone instability in Hainanese
(Yun 1987: 14–23, Wee 2020)

In isolation	When followed by another syllable
toiʔ 'wash' | low	toiʔ biʔ 'wash the rice' | | high low
	toiʔ fiue 'wash the flowers' | | high high
mak 'eye(s)' | falling	mak tai 'in front of eyes/presently' | | low mid
fiiʔ 'ear' | falling	fiiʔ ʔuat 'ear pick' | | low falling

sandhi. There are also cases of tone deletion (e.g., Standard Chinese, Chao 1948, 1968), and of movement (e.g., in Chizigula, see Section 4.1).

This section has outlined that complexities of tone come from a number of factors. Firstly, they interface with morphosyntactic entities. At the word level, tone yields lexical contrasts. They can also be applied to other aspects of grammar to signal grammatical case and intonation. Secondly, tones may signal prosodic differences. This is an area that has recently caught the attention of many tonologists. Thirdly, tone is unstable and can change forms and positions. Tones can be inserted, deleted, and spread (Goldsmith 1976, Gussenhoven 2004, Wee 2019, Hyman and Leben 2020). Subsequent sections will deal with these topics in turn all of which lead us to the need for rather complex structures in the representation of tone.

2 The Physical Dimensions of Tone

The reader will notice that in any discussion of tone, labels like 'high', 'low', 'rising', 'falling', 'dipping', 'peaking', and so on, are really just spatial metaphors to describe the perceived melodic shapes. The same kind of metaphor is used for musical melodies, corresponding to the psychoacoustic concept of 'pitch'. By connecting linguistic tone to pitch, one looks in the direction of physical properties such as fundamental frequency (F0) and the vocal folds which produce F0 in speech. In reality, the physics of tone will involve intensity, duration, and other acoustic properties as well, in relation to the human articulatory systems. Through an overview of the physical dimensions of tone, this section hopes to reveal some of the complexities that are less often studied.

2.1 Pitch Perception

It is worth remembering that before recording technologies were conveniently available, fieldwork investigations relied on pitch perception for the description of tone, drawing analogies with music. For example, Low (1828) laid out Thai tones according to a system based on a treble clef, and Pallegoix (1854) marked each Thai tone as a literal melody in Western musical notation. The most notable of such works might be Chao's (1930) system of tone letters, where the numbers 1–5 produce a scale ranging from very low to very high. Any tone contour can thus be captured by a series of such tone values, say [51] is a full falling tone and [35] is a mid rising tone. Level tones can be represented with two identical numbers, for example, [55] would be a very high flat tone. Chao explicitly acknowledged inspiration from music, pointing out that one could imagine [1] to [5] as analogous to the musical interval known as the perfect fifth (e.g., C to G, or D to A). However, Chao added that a linguistic tone may not align itself so squarely with any particular music interval, and recommended that [1] simply represents the lowest pitch level in normal speech and [5] the highest. Chao's foresight is borne out by later studies, which show that the interval spans do indeed vary widely across speakers in different languages, as seen in Table 9.

As technology has become more affordable, field investigations can now be readily substantiated by recordings and tone descriptions informed by detailed acoustic measurements (such as Zhang and Liu 2011, 2016, among others) (more in Section 2.3). At the same time, analysts usually use a combination of approximate pitch perception, logarithmic-adjusted and normalized F0 profile measurements, and phonological contrast in their description of tones, instead of relying exclusively on acoustic details. In any case, field data published from longer ago would rely more on the ear of the linguist than on instrumental measurement and analysis. To the extent that the descriptions lend themselves to phonological understanding, ears and machinery should both be brought to bear on the subject. After all, the perceived tone is not necessarily a direct mapping of F0, and the perception of pitch can be affected by a listener's native phonological system.

2.2 Physiology

On account of the importance of F0, tonal production relies largely on the control of the vocal folds. The vocal folds are connected at one end to the thyroid cartilage and at the other to the arytenoid cartilages. Adduction (closing)

Table 9 Pitch ranges of speakers in twenty Chinese languages (Wee 2017)

Language	Gender	F0 range of lowest pitch (Hz)	F0 range of highest pitch (Hz)	High-Low quotient (median values)
Túnxī 屯溪 (Hui)	F	135–152	245	1.71
Méixiàn 梅縣 (Hakka)	F	144–149	267–278	1.86
Nánníng 南寧 (Yue)	F	120	180–268	1.87
Taipei 台北 (S. Min)	F	92–173	253	1.91
Fúzhōu 福州 (N. Min)	F	116–142	252	1.95
Hǎikǒu 海口 (S. Min)	M	78–92	160–176	1.98
Wēnzhōu 溫州 (Wu)	M	149–152	294–303	1.98
Hong Kong 香港 (Yue)	F	149	282–325	2.04
Táoyuán 桃園 (Mandarin)	M	75–89	163–173	2.05
Jiàn'ōu 建甌 (N. Min)	F	135–145	301–302	2.15
Sūzhōu 蘇州 (Wu)	F	129–161	289–350	2.20
Shàntóu 汕頭 (S. Min)	F	143–150	316–379	2.37
Shèxiàn 歙縣 (Hui)	F	134–150	338	2.38
Xiāngtán 湘潭 (Xiang)	F	145–167	371	2.38
Xiàmén 廈門 (S. Min)	M	75	181	2.41

Table 9 (cont.)

Language	Gender	F0 range of lowest pitch (Hz)	F0 range of highest pitch (Hz)	High-Low quotient (median values)
Hángzhōu 杭州 (Wu)	M	76–131	256	2.47
Shànghǎi 上海 (Wu)	M	75–79	193	2.51
Nánchāng 南昌 (Gan)	M	75–82	187–213	2.55
Guǎngzhōu 廣州 (Yue)	M	75–80	200–218	2.70
Chángshā 長沙 (Xiang)	M	75–113	290	3.09

Music interval	Corresponding High-Low quotient*	Musical interval	Corresponding High-Low quotient
Major second	1.122462	Minor second	1.059463
Major third	1.259921	Minor third	1.189207
Perfect fifth	1.498307	Perfect fourth	1.334839
Major sixth	1.681792	Minor sixth	1.587401
Major seventh	1.887748	Minor seventh	1.781797
Octave	2		

* Quotients for music intervals based on twelve-tone equal temperament, which uses $2^{n/12}$, an irrational number, as a multiplier.

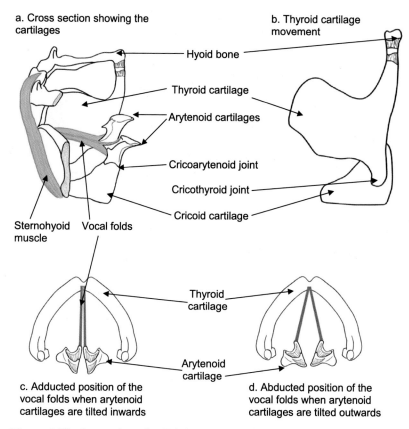

a. Cross section showing the cartilages

Hyoid bone

Thyroid cartilage

Arytenoid cartilages

Cricoarytenoid joint

Cricothyroid joint

Cricoid cartilage

Sternohyoid muscle   Vocal folds

b. Thyroid cartilage movement

Thyroid cartilage

Arytenoid cartilage

c. Adducted position of the vocal folds when arytenoid cartilages are tilted inwards

d. Abducted position of the vocal folds when arytenoid cartilages are tilted outwards

Figure 1 The larynx (see also Erickson 1976, Ohala 1978, Erickson *et al.* 1995)
Images by Winnie H. Y. Cheung

and abduction (opening) are controlled by the tilting of the arytenoid cartilages inwards or outwards (see Figure 1).

In the adducted position, the vocal folds allow pressure to build up as air is pushed out of the lungs. Vibration results through repeated bouts of air release through the vocal folds to produce F0. Through control of the arytenoid cartilages, the folds may be made tighter to create higher frequencies or looser to create lower frequencies. However, for very low frequencies, the sternohyoid muscle (Figure 1a) will have to pull the thyroid cartilage downwards to lengthen the vocal folds (Ohala and Hirose 1970, Ohala 1972, although see Niimi, Horiguchi, and Kobayashi 1991 for how the sternohyoid can be used to raise F0 in singing as well, albeit not in speech). In articulatory terms, this means that mid tones are easiest to produce, followed by high tones, then low tones. This concept will become very relevant when one looks at how many levels of tone-height contrast are found in different languages (see Section 3).

Table 10 Tone inventories of Jinxing Bai exhibiting phonation

Normally phonated	Specially phonated
[55]	[66] tensed
[33]	[44] tensed
[31]	[42] glottalized
[35] (loanwords only)	[21] tense/creaky, fricated

The fundamental frequency may not be the only parameter relevant for tone (Andruski and Ratliff 2000, Kuo, Rosen, and Faulkner 2008, Brunelle 2009, Garellek *et al.* 2013). Vietnamese, for example, requires glottalization to contrast between two tones that are otherwise quite similar in terms of their perceived pitch: the *sắc* 'sharp' tone and the *ngã* 'tumbling' tone are both described as mid rising, but the latter has an intervening glottal (Nguyen and Edmondson 1997: 8 and Pham 2003: 57). Similarly, Hudak (2008) observed that certain tones are glottalized across Tai languages. Wang's (2012: 41–5) fieldwork uncovered four different dialects of Bai in which voice quality was an important aspect of their tonal inventory. One of these is reproduced in Table 10.

The specific voicing qualities of these Bai cases require further study. In any case, issues of voice quality in relation to tone can be tricky. Even with appeal to minimal pairs, one may still find it hard to ascertain whether specifics of phonation should be attributed to differences in the vocalic segments or to tone (Andruski and Ratliff 2000, Garellek *et al.* 2013). This difficulty is particularly evident for the connection between segmental properties and tone in terms of tonogenesis (Thurgood 2007, Brunelle and Kirby 2016, Gehrmann and Dockum 2021).

2.3 Acoustics

Given the early emphasis on pitch in the study of tone, the most obvious acoustic correlate would be F0. It is on this basis that much research focuses exclusively on F0 patterns in tone description, but one should note that human perception and processing of linguistic tone may be due to a composite of different acoustic cues (Andruski and Ratliff 2000, Kuo *et al.* 2008, Brunelle 2009, Garellek *et al.* 2013, Kuang 2013).

A case for F0 can be seen in the rather neat match between traditional descriptions of tone contours and the F0 tracks in Standard Chinese, which is said to have four lexical tones (Table 11).

As per the system in Chao (1930), T(one) 1 is a high flat tone [55], T2 a rising tone [35], T3 a dipping tone [214] and T4 a falling tone [51]. Figure 2 offers the time-normalized (using Xu 2013) F0 profiles of each tone averaged from six

Table 11 Standard Chinese tones

	Description	Tone values	Examples
Tone 1	High flat	[55]	ma_{55} 'mother', ti_{55} 'kick', fu_{55} 'husband'
Tone 2	Rising	[35]	ma_{35} 'hemp', ti_{35} 'hoof', fu_{35} 'fortune'
Tone 3	Dipping	[214]	ma_{214} 'horse', ti_{214} 'body', fu_{214} 'rot'
Tone 4	Falling	[51]	ma_{51} 'scold', ti_{51} 'shave', fu_{51} 'father'

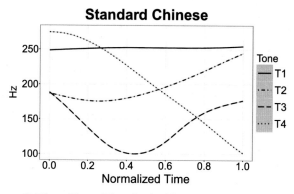

Figure 2 F0 profiles of Standard Chinese (from Wee 2019: 11)
Image reproduced with permission from author.

recordings by a female native speaker (twenty-eight years old). To ensure statistical validity, SSANOVA was applied at a 95-per-cent confidence interval around each spline to produce a ribbon for each set of recordings for every tone. As can be seen, the F0 profiles generally match the tone values, although one can be picky and argue that T3 should perhaps be revised as [313] or that T1 should be [44] in view of the fact that T4 begins higher. These nitty-gritty details are probably irrelevant, and are excessive if what is relevant are the general shapes and perhaps a simple two- to three-way distinction for height.

The F0 profile in Figure 2 is time normalized, which masks differences in the duration of each tone. From the same recordings of the same speaker, we have the time measurements shown in Table 12.

Given the relatively small standard deviations, the durations are presumably consistent for each tone, despite token differences. Tone 3 is obviously longer than the rest, although one could concede that compared to F0, duration would be a much poorer cue, but a cue nonetheless should F0 be suppressed (as in whispering for instance) (Abramson 1972, Chang and Yao 2007, Heeren 2015).

Intensity can come into play as well, as reported in Fu and Zeng (2000). Figure 3 gives an illustration of the intensity profiles of tones in Standard Chinese, which corroborates the observation in Fu and Zeng (2000).

Table 12 Durations of Standard Chinese tones (from Wee 2019: 11)

Length of T(one) 1 [55]	= 0.537s	StdDev=0.095
Length of T2 [25]	= 0.582s	StdDev=0.068
Length of T3 [214]	= 0.660s	StdDev=0.045
Length of T4 [51]	= 0.519s	StdDev=0.075

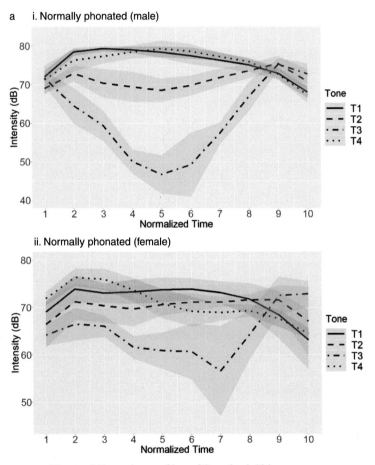

Figure 3 Intensity profiles of Standard Chinese tones

Figure 3 offers time-normalized (again, using Xu 2013) intensity profiles of each tone. Five tokens are recorded for each tone by a male native speaker and a female speaker (both forty-three years old) who produced them first normally phonated, then in a whisper. The shared ribbons indicate the deviation within a 95-per-cent confidence level. Looking first at Figure 3a, the intensity profiles for the male

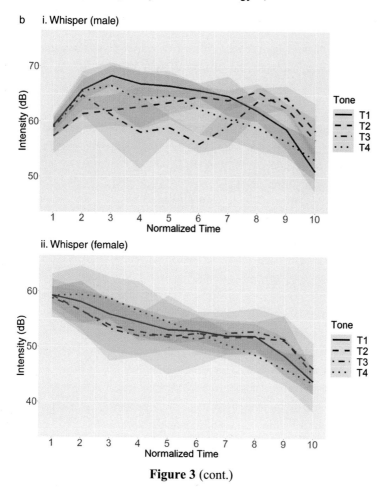

Figure 3 (cont.)

speaker are quite distinct for Tones 2 and 3, although Tones 1 and 4 seem to overlap. For the female speaker, only Tone 3 is clearly distinct. In whispers, the overlap of the intensity profiles for both speakers suggests that intensity may no longer be a very reliable cue, although for the male speaker Tone 3 remains quite distinct. The distinctive intensity profile of Tone 3 was also reported in Gao (2002: section 4). Thus, acoustically, there are indeed more correlates than just F0 for tone.

Other than the details of physiology and acoustics, the main takeaway of this section is that phonetics of tone is itself a complex subject. Many of its tonal correlates apply to stress as well. While phonetics can give much grounding to the complex patterns, we must take on board Ladefoged's (1997: 138) reminder that 'The first requirement for a phonetic description of a language is a good account of the phonology'. It is to phonology that we now turn.

3 Tonal Transcription and Inventories

We now turn to the complexities associated with transcribing and representing tones, and the theoretical issues that arise with attempts to do so.

3.1 Tone Values and Features

That pitch is the ostensible character of linguistic tone makes systems such as Chao's (1930) tone values (he called them 'tone letters') the most convenient (see Table 13).

While shafts and contours may be more iconic, the symbols are harder to type. The same difficulty plagues the use of accent marks on vowels, which have the added obstacle of being difficult to read. In some studies, particularly those relating to tones in South American languages (e.g., Trique, in Hollenbach 1988 and 2008: 12), the numbers are used in reverse, with [1] being the highest and [5] the lowest. For consistency, this Element will adopt Chao's system, indicating them in subscript, for example [ma$_{51}$]. (Tone indications in most published literature are often given superscripts, which we find creates the potential for them to be confused with the indices for foot- or endnotes.)

Although handy, Chao's transcription system offers a logical possibility of 5 different tone heights, 20 different rises and falls, and 100 types of peaks and dips, totalling an inventory of 125 tone value combinations (5 x 5 x 5 = 125). This seems excessive for phonological representations of tone; there are no known languages with a tone inventory quite as large, as the following examples from Han Chinese languages demonstrate (Table 14).

Wang (1967) observed that Chao's system may veil important similarities between the languages, and many later researchers reduced the numerals into notations such as H(igh), L(ow), F(alling), R(ising) (Dockum 2018). For example,

Table 13 Common transcription systems for tones

	Chao's (1930) tone values	Shaft and contour	Vowel accent marks
Very high	[55]	˥	a̋
High	[44]	˦	á
Mid	[33]	˧	ā
Low	[22]	˨	à
Very low	[11]	˩	ȁ
Full falling	[51]		â
Full rising	[15]		ǎ
High peaking	[353]		᷈a
Low dipping	[313]		

Table 14 Tone inventories from some Han Chinese
languages (Beijing 1989: 7–45)

Group	Language	Level	Falling	Rising	Dipping	Peaking
Mandarin	Jǐnán	55	42, 21		213	
	Xī'ān	55	53, 21	24		
	Tàiyuán	11	53	45		
	Wǔhàn	55	42	35	213	
	Chéngdū	44	53, 31	13		
	Héféi	55	53	24	212	
	Yángzhōu	55	42, 21	34		
Wu	Sūzhōu	44	31	24	412	
	Wēnzhōu	44, 22	42, 31	45, 34	323, 212	
Xiang	Chángshā	55, 33	41, 21	24, 13		
	Shuāngfēng	55, 33	21	35, 23		
Gan	Nánchāng		42, 21	45, 24	213	
Hakka	Méixiàn	44, 11	52, 31			
Yue	Yángjiāng	33	54, 43, 21	24		
Min	Cháozhōu	55, 33, 11	53	35	213	
	Fúzhōu	44	52, 31		213	242
	Jiàn'ōu	44, 22	54, 42, 21	24		

eight different inventories were documented from different sites in Jiangsu, but appear really to be superfluous complexities (see Table 15).

The finesse of the tone values masks the commonalities of the profiles of each tone given in the final row of Table 15. As one of the first attempts to generalize over the details of tones, Wang (1967) proposed a set of binary features that would allow corresponding tones in the different dialects to have the same phonological representation, arguing that a better capture of the tonal phonology might be enabled by the use of tone features, shown in Table 16.

Wang did not provide definitions for each of the features, but through this table one could discern what they represent. Binary values for each feature and a three-way distinction for height [high, central, mid] yield a five-way contrast for tone heights as illustrated in the five columns for [55] to [11]. Thus, if indeed there were tonal languages that require that many contrasts for level tones, the system would be adequate. Maddieson (1978, see also Edmondson and

Table 15 Tone data from eight sites in Jiangsu (Wang 1967)

	Tone 1	Tone 2	Tone 3	Tone 4
Site a	213			52
Site b	212		35	
Site c		55		51
Site d	313			
Site e				52
Site f		54	24	
Site g	213			51
Site h		55		42
Profile	Dipping	High	Rising	Falling

Table 16 Wang's (1967) tone features

	55	44	33	22	11	35	13	53	31	535	313	353	131
[contour]	−	−	−	−	−	+	+	+	+	+	+	+	+
[high]	+	+	−	−	−	+	−	+	−	+	−	+	−
[central]	−	+	+	+	−	−	−	−	−	−	−	−	−
[mid]	−	−	+	−	−	−	−	−	−	−	−	−	−
[rising]	−	−	−	−	−	+	+	−	−	+	+	+	+
[falling]	−	−	−	−	−	−	−	+	+	+	+	+	+
[convex]	−	−	−	−	−	−	−	−	−	−	−	+	+

Gregerson 1992 for a more recent study) provides the following list of such languages. However, it should be noted that five-level contrasts in many languages have also been shown to involve non-modal phonations (Kuang 2013 for Black Miao) or glottalizations (Sarawit 1975 on Puyi languages).

Languages with five tone heights (augmenting Maddieson 1978)
• Dan (a Mande language, Bearth and Zemp 1967)
• Kporo and Ashuku (both Mbembe languages, Shimizu 1971)
• Ngamambo (a Grassfields Bantoid language, Asongwed and Hyman 1977)
• Black Miao (data from F. K. Li, cited by Chang 1953 and Voegelin and Voegelin 1965; corroborated in Wang 1967; Kwan 1971, Shi 1987, Shi, Shi, and Liao 1987)
• Tahua Yao (a Mienic language, Chang 1953)
• Some of the Puyi (also spelt Bouyei, Buyi) dialects (Tai-Kadai languages, Sarawit 1973, 1975)
• Trique (Longacre 1952; Hollenbach 1988, 2008, Matsukawa 2012)
• Ticuna (a Tichuna-Yuri language, Anderson 1959; Anderson 1962)
• Usila Chinantec (a Ojitlan language, Rensch 1968; Suárez 1983: 51)

With tone features, the superfluous distinction between [213] and [313] in Jiangsu would disappear, both being [+contour, +rising, +falling, -high, -convex]. The same principle applies to the other tones, thus capturing the commonality in the tonal inventories of the eight different sites in Table 15.

Wang's approach is a milestone in understanding the complexity of tones precisely because the features pierce through the cloud of details that might be systemically irrelevant. Nonetheless, obvious redundancies prompted Wang to offer the following conventions in the same paper.

Redundancy conventions (Wang 1967)

a. [-contour] → [-rising, -falling, -convex]

b. $\left\{ \begin{array}{l} [+high] \\ [-central] \end{array} \right\}$ → [-mid]

c. [+central] → [-contour]

d. $\left\{ \begin{array}{l} [+rising] \\ [+falling] \end{array} \right\}$ → [+contour]

e. [+contour] → [-central, -mid]

f. $\left\{ \begin{array}{l} [-rising] \\ [-falling] \end{array} \right\}$ → [-convex]

Most redundancies are logical, as for example, anything that is [-contour] is flat and therefore [-rising], [-falling], and [-convex]. Others are probably stipulative, for example the fact that [+contour] is [-central] leads one to wonder whether there are to be distinctions in languages where a rising tone might have three levels of contrast. A challenging case might come from the San Juan Copala dialect of Trique (as reported in Hollenbach 1988, 2008: 12).

San Juan Copala (Trique)

yã₁₁ 'one (in certain number phrases)'
yã₂₂ 'unmarried'
yã₃₃ 'he is sitting'
yã₃₂ 'salt'
yã₃₁ 'scar'
yã₁₃ 'Spanish moss'
yã₃₄ 'corncob'
yã₄₅ 'to be sitting'

In San Juan Copala, [13], [34], and [45] are contrastive. This would either require review of the redundancy convention relating [central] or [mid] to [contour] for Wang's system or else perhaps considering [45] as a high-level

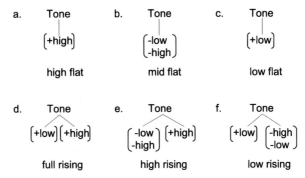

Figure 4 Simple tone-feature concatenation

Table 17 Tones as articulatory features

Woo (1969)	[high]	[low]	
	+	-	High tone
	-	-	Mid tone
	-	+	Low tone
Halle and Stevens (1971)	[stiff]	[slack]	

tone in the language, thus removing the three-way contrast for rising tones. Until there is evidence one way or another, this has to remain an open question.

Wang (1967) gave reason for a unitary treatment of tones as opposed to just pitch values. In the same decade, Woo (1969) suggested that perhaps a simple two-feature system that uses [high] and [low] would suffice if contoured tones can be treated as a concatenation of features.

The tones from Figure (4a–f) would respectively be high flat, mid flat, low flat, full rising, high rising, and low rising. Such a view implies that tone contours are composite, and has the added advantage of requiring fewer features and also fewer redundancies. Woo's system later found greater development through the work of Yip (1980) and Bao (1990). In the meantime, there was to be a further attempt at a reduction on how tone works, this time from Halle and Stevens (1971) who sought to find articulatory bases for the tone features. By appealing to [stiff] and [slack] features that describe the state of the vocal folds, Halle and Stevens' system engendered the possibility for tones to be treated similarly with other distinctive features such as [voice], [nasal], [labial]. Woo's system can be easily translated to that of Halle and Stevens, as shown in Table 17.

Whichever way one may wish to describe tones, the choice must be empirically motivated. Following Wang's (1967) lead, a good angle would be to consider inventories that need to be captured. In this aspect, Yip (1980) and

Table 18 Traditional tone categories in Standard Cantonese

Middle Chinese category		Tone value	Example	Remarks
Ping	Yin	[55]	[ji$_{55}$] 'clothes'	
	Yang	[21]	[ji$_{21}$] 'child'	
Shang	Yin	[35]	[ji$_{35}$] 'chair'	
	Yang	[13]	[ji$_{13}$] 'ear'	
Qu	Yin	[33]	[ji$_{33}$] 'meaning'	
	Yang	[22]	[ji$_{22}$] 'two'	
Ru	Yin-a	[5]	[jik$_5$] 'beneficial'	Only found in syllables closed by obstruents [p, t, k]
	Yin-b	[3]	[jip$_3$] 'marinade'	
	Yang	[2]	[jik$_2$] 'wings' [jip$_2$] 'page'	

Bao (1990) offered critical evidence that would lead to the establishment of the tone register, the subject of the ensuing subsection (3.2).

3.2 Hidden Dividers: Tone Register

After reviewing Chao's tone values and the different features of Wang's, Woo's, and Halle and Stevens', we move for the moment to tone inventories. The Standard Cantonese tone inventory had, following philological traditions, been said to have nine different tones, an inventory inherited from Middle Chinese (see Table 18).

The Middle Chinese tone-category names come from antiquity, and have been in use since at least the fifth century CE. They may have once been descriptive labels of the tone contours (*Ping* 'level', *Shang* 'up', *Qu* 'departing', and *Ru* 'entering'), but these are all now speculative. The Ru tones are all short, hence the use of a single tone value, which correlates with the fact that they appear only with syllables closed by voiceless plosives. It is thus reasonable to suggest that perhaps each different Ru tone is the result of the plosive coda masking the second half of the tone melody of one of the other six tones. Taking this cue, and sorting the tones in terms of the Yin and Yang subcategories, a pattern emerges, as in Table 19.

Yip (1980) noticed that Cantonese appears to have divided the tonal space into an upper pitch range (here corresponding to the *Yin* subcategory) and a lower one (here, the *Yang* subcategory). Within each range, there would be a high tone, a low tone, and a rising tone. A little licence is needed to regard [21] as a low flat tone rather than a falling tone, which may be granted if one recognizes that reaching the

Table 19 Cantonese tones by 'register'

	Yin	**Yang**
High	55	22
Rising	35	13
Low	33	21
Register	Upper	Lower

Table 20 Tone inventory of Songjiang (Bao 1999: 12)

Tone	**Example**	**Unattested forms**
[53]	tʰi 'ladder' ti 'low'	*di
[31]	di 'lift'	*tʰi, *ti
[44]	tʰi 'body' ti 'bottom'	*di
[22]	di 'brother'	*tʰi, *ti
[35]	tʰi 'tear' ti 'emperor'	*di
[13]	di 'field'	*tʰi, *ti
[5]	pʰaʔ 'tap' paʔ 'hundred'	*baʔ
[3]	baʔ 'white'	*pʰaʔ, *paʔ

very low pitch target requires an extra pull of the sternohyoid muscle (recall Figure 1a). Thusly, [21] is presumably an aberration of the intended [11] target. That *Yin* should correspond to the upper register and *Yang* to the lower is not incidental, but historically triggered by the voicing properties of onset consonants (more later in Section 7.2). The concept of register calls into question Wang's (1967) [high] feature, which served the dual purpose of (i) describing a high level (corresponding to [55] and [44]) and (ii) indicating the range of tones (distinguishing [35] from [13], although [33] itself is [-high] in Wang's system).

Bao's (1999, recast from 1990) description of languages like Songjiang and Chaozhou offers reasons in favour of Yip's 'register'. In Songjiang, there is a covariation between the voicing of the onset and the tone register (Table 20).

Songjiang is interesting in that there is an interaction between the [voice] feature of the onset and the tone, which calls to mind Halle and Stevens' (1971) attempt at relating tone features with other distinctive features. More directly relevant is that the pattern of Songjiang motivates the possible division of pitch range within the tonal space. This concept of pitch range is to be distinguished from the features that describe the tonal contour, and must not be collapsed into the same dimension, as Wang did.

Table 21 Register agreement in Chaozhou tone (Cai 1991: 5, Bao 1999: 81–2)

Phrase-final tone	Before [53, 55, 5]	Before [33, 213, 11, 2]
[53]	[35]	[24]
[213]	[53]	[42]

Examples

hue	[53]		'fire'
hue	[35]	ba [53]	'fire-hold (torch)'
hue	[35]	lou [55]	'fire-heath (stove)'
hue	[35]	tsiʔ [5]	'fire-tongue (flame)'
hue	[24]	suã [33]	'fire-mountain (volcano)'
hue	[24]	tsĩ [213]	'fire-arrow (rocket)'
hue	[24]	tsʰiu [11]	'fire-tree'
hue	[24]	sok [2]	'fire-speed (speedy)'

hue	[213]		'product'
hue	[53]	kʰuaŋ [53]	'product-term (payment)'
hue	[53]	luŋ [55]	'product-wheel (freight ship)'
hue	[53]	mueʔ [5]	'product'
hue	[42]	tsʰŋ [33]	'product-store (warehouse)'
hue	[42]	ke [213]	'product-price'
hue	[42]	iõ [11]	'product-appearance (sample)'
hue	[42]	sek [2]	'product-colour (quality)'

The case for the need of an independent tone register is strengthened by register spreading in Chaozhou. In Chaozhou, a tone associated with a syllable-sized morpheme undergoes alternation when in a non-phrase-final position, a property common among Southern Min languages (Table 21).

From Table 21, one can see that the falling tone of Chaozhou *hue* 'fire' [53] alternates to become a rising tone. This derived rising tone varies between [35] and [24] depending on whether the following tone belongs to the higher or lower pitch ranges. With *hue* [213] 'product', the derived tone is falling, and is either [53] and [42], similarly sensitive to the following tone's pitch range. In other words, Chaozhou exhibits tone register agreement.

The postulation of register makes explicable the otherwise mysterious phenomenon of tone leaping seen in Ewe (see Figure 5).

The accent marks in Figure 5 indicate tone: ē is mid, é is high, and e̋ is a raised/extra high. Of particular interest is the mid tone *mēg-* in *mēgbé* 'behind'. When sandwiched by two high tones (5b, c), *mēg* leaps higher than its neighbours to

a. /ākplɔ̄ mēgbé/   →   [ākplɔ̄ mēgbé]   'behind a spear'
b. /ētō mēgbé/   →   [ētō mɛ̋gbé]   'behind a mortar'
c. /ēkpé mēgbé/   →   [ēkpé mɛ̋gbé]   'behind a stone'

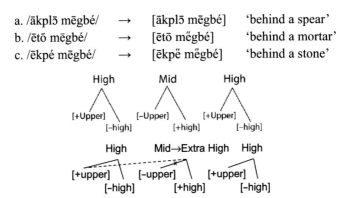

Figure 5 Ewe tone leap (Odden 1995, see also Clements 1978)

Note: an animated version of the figure is available in the online resources (www.cambridge
.org/wee-li).

become *mɛ̋g*. A straightforward explanation is possible if there is a [+upper] register
that spreads and displaces the register of the mid tone [-upper, +high]. This would
make for the extra high [+upper, +high], as illustrated in Figure 5.

With tone register, inventories that appear haphazard may now reveal their
symmetries. As already seen in Cantonese, the six tones are simply the result of
having two registers apply to high, low, and rising tones. In Songjiang, the
inventory in Table 20 can now be understood and recast as Table 22.

The short tones in Songjiang are found only with syllables closed by the
glottal [ʔ], and need to be treated as a difference in syllable type rather than in
tone category, as already explained for Cantonese.

Sometimes, the effect of tone register may not be evident from a simple study of a
language's tonal inventory, as exemplified in the Northern Wu dialect of Hangzhou.

In Table 23, one can see a hint of tone register in Hangzhou; as with
Songjiang, the voicing of onsets appears to co-vary with the *Yin* and *Yang*
subcategories of tone. Possibly, in Hsieh's (2008) transcription, there also
seem to be two different kinds of rising tones [24] and [14]. However, since
the tones do not obviously sort themselves into contrasting pairs of rising or
falling tones to match differences in register, the evidence for register in
Hangzhou (i.e., voicing complementarity of onsets) appears to be external to
tonology. We shall return to Hsieh's study later in Section 3.3, and will presently
focus on Xu's data. In Xu's report, evidence for register in Hangzhou can be
extracted from patterns of tonal collocation. When tones are concatenated in
Hangzhou, they undergo a rather complex tone sandhi (i.e., alternation). To see
tone register at work, what is needed is a simple comparison between the older
and newer varieties of the Hangzhou dialect, as in Table 24.

Table 22 Tone inventory of Songjiang (Bao 1999: 12)

	Upper	Lower
Falling	[53]	[31]
Rising	[35]	[13]
Flat	[44] / [5]	[22] / [3]

Table 23 Tone inventory of Hangzhou

Middle Chinese category		Tone value (Xu 2007)	Tone value (Hsieh 2008)	Example
Ping	Yin	[33]	[44]	tsʮ 'red'
	Yang	[213]	[24]	dzʮ 'remove'
Shang	Yin	[53]	[51]	tsʮ 'lord'
Qu	Yin	[445]	[34]	tsʮ 'rot'
	Yang	[13]	[14]	dzʮ 'stay'
Ru	Yin	[5]	[4]	sʮəʔ 'say'
	Yang	[2]	[24]	zʮəʔ 'hot'

Table 24 Tone sandhi of Hangzhou (Xu 2007)

		-[33]	-[53]	-[445]	-[213]	-[13]
[33]-	Old	33–33				
	New	33–35			33–13	
[53]-	Old	43–53				
	New	53–43			53–21	
[445]-	Old	44–21				
	New	35–53			35–31	
[213]-	Old	11–33	11–53	11–35	11–33	
	New	11–35			11–13	
[13]-	Old	13–53				
	New	13–53			13–31	

In Table 24, we have omitted the Ru tones which occur only when syllables are closed by glottal stops. The table is plotted so that tones given along the first column are followed by tones given along the top row. The concatenation triggers alternation as for example, among the older variety of Hangzhou, a concatenation of [33] with any tone produces [33–33], preserving the tone of the first syllable and neutralizing the second all to [33]. When [53] is followed by any tone, the result is [43]–[53] for that same variety. Ignoring for the moment the concatenation of [213]–, a clear distinction between the older and newer varieties is that the newer variety splits the tones in the second syllable into two subgroups: -[33], -[53], and -[445] in one group and -[213] and -[13] in the other. This bifurcation of tones in the newer variety applies also to [213]- concatenations, yielding either [11–35] or [11–13] depending on the following tone. Evidently, the newer variety of Hangzhou is register sensitive (matching the *Yin* and *Yang* subcategories), and the registers of the second tone are preserved even if the tone contours alternate. That register sensitivity does not apply to the older variety.

Both Songjiang and Hangzhou belong to the Wu cluster of Han Chinese, and symmetries of register can be found in other languages as well. Bai, whose familial ties have been variously debated to be Tibeto-Burman or Sino-Tibetan, offers a remote enough case on register splits in tone inventories. Here are the inventories of five Bai dialects, all of which exhibit very neat register bifurcation (Table 25).

The relationship between these five Bai dialects should be quite evident, so that from their differences, one might be able to construct the tone inventory of their common ancestor, which would very likely include register symmetries.

3.3 Compositionality of Tone Melodies

Recall in Figure 4 the idea that tone contours are composed of smaller atomic features that cannot be further analysed. Support for such a view may be found in languages such as Kukuya (Table 26) and Mende (Table 27). In both languages, the general tone profile of words, mono- or polysyllabic regardless, may either be high flat, low flat, falling, rising, or peaking.

Ignoring the bracketed prefixes in Kukuya, one will notice that for disyllabic words, rising tones and falling tones do not appear in the same syllable. Instead the entire tone contour seems to be broken up and spread across two syllables. Peaking tones likewise appear to spread out across each syllable in trisyllabic words. The patterns are easily discernible from how the complex tone accent marks in monosyllabic forms split up in the polysyllabic ones. These patterns would be most easily explained if tone contours were the result of concatenation of atomic tone features such as [high] and [low]. In all cases, it is a simple matter

Table 25 Tone inventories of five Bai dialects exhibiting register splits (Wang 2012: 36–41)

a. Tuoluo Bai

	Level	Falling	Rising
Upper	[55]	[42]	[35]
Lower	[33]	[21]	

b. Gongxing Bai

	Level	Falling	Rising
Upper	[55]	[42]	[24]
Lower	[22]	[21]	[12]

c. Enqi Bai

	Level	Falling	Rising
Upper	[55]	[43]	[24]
Lower	[22]	[21]	

d. Ega Bai

	Level	Falling
Upper	[55]	[42]
	[44]	
Lower	[22]	[21]

e. Jinman Bai

	Level	Falling
Upper	[55]	[42]
Lower	[22]	[21]

of assigning the tone features rightwards to each syllable until the tones and/or syllables are exhausted, akin to Figure 6, where each t stands for a tone feature.

This treatment for Kukuya and Mende extends to suffixation, lending more weight to the hypothesis. In Table 28 below, we can see that the tones spread to the toneless suffixes in a way consistent with the schemata given in Figure 6.

Table 26 Word tones in Kukuya (Hyman 1987, with data from Paulian 1974)

	Tone	Monosyllabic	Disyllabic	Trisyllabic
i.	High	(mà).bá 'oil palms'	(mà).bágá 'show knives'	(kì).bálágá 'fence'
ii.	Low	(kì).bà 'grasshopper killer'	(kì).bàlà 'to build'	(kì).bàlàgà 'to change route'
iii.	Falling	(kì).kâ 'to pick'	(kì).kárà 'paralytic'	(kì).káràgà 'not be entangled'
iv.	Rising	(mù).sǎ 'weaving knot'	(mù).sàmí 'conversation'	.mʷàrəgí 'younger brother'
v.	Peaking	(.ndɛ́)bvî 'he falls'	(.ndɛ́)pàlî 'he goes out'	(.ndɛ́)kàlə́gì 'he turns around'

Table 27 Word tones in Mende (Leben 1973: 64, 1978; see also Leben 2017 for nuances)

	Tone	Monosyllabic	Disyllabic	Trisyllabic
i.	High	kɔ́ 'weapon'	pɛ́lɛ́ 'house'	pɛ́lɛ́-má 'on house'
ii.	Low	kpà 'debt'	bɛ̀lɛ̀ 'trousers'	bɛ̀lɛ̀-hù 'in trousers'
iii.	Falling	mbû 'owl'	kényà 'uncle'	ŋgílà-mà 'on dog'
iv.	Rising	mbǎ 'rice'	nìká 'cow'	nìká-má 'on cow'
v.	Peaking	mbā 'companion'	nyàhâ 'woman'	nìkílì 'peanut'

Table 28 Tone patterns in Mende polymorphemic nouns (Leben 1978)

	Tone	Citation	-hu 'in'	-ma 'on'	Gloss
i.	L	bɛ̀lɛ̀	bɛ̀lɛ̀-hù	bɛ̀lɛ̀-mà	'trousers'
ii.	H	kɔ́	kɔ́-hú	kɔ́-má	'war'
		pɛ́lɛ́	pɛ́lɛ́-hú	pɛ́lɛ́-má	'house'
iii.	LH	mbǎ	mbà-hú	mbà-má	'rice'
iv.	HL	mbû	mbú-hù	mbú-mà	'owl'
		ŋgílà	ŋgílà-hù	ŋgílà-mà	'dog'
v.	LHL	ɲàhâ	ɲàhá-hù	ɲàhá-mà	'woman'

This Kukuya/Mende-style of tone spreading appears to be quite common. It is also found in Shanghainese, for example (Shih 1986). While languages like Kukuya and Mende argue for the compositionality of contoured tones, Hangzhou offers an interesting counterargument. Recall that in Table 23 there

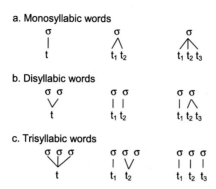

Figure 6 Tone assignment in Kukuya and Mende

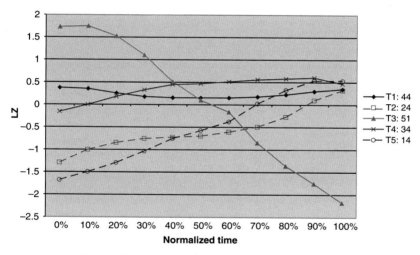

Figure 7 Tone melodies in Hangzhou (Hsieh 2008)

Image reproduced with permission from the author.

were two different studies on Hangzhou tones. Xu's (2007) inventory and that of Hsieh (2008) appear to be quite different. We are not sure whether the differences arose out of there being different subdialects, and shall therefore take both as equally valid. Hsieh cited Qian (1992), Simmons (1992), and Bao (1998) as his sources, and offered pitch extractions from recordings by Bao (2003). Hsieh's pitch tracks are given in Figure 7.

Citing earlier works such as Chen (2000: 320–5), Hsieh began by first noting that a disyllabic string in Hangzhou typically undergoes tone sandhi by first deleting the tone of the second syllable and then spreading the tone of the first, not unlike Kukuya or Mende. This is also the general pattern of Northern Wu languages, of which Shanghai and Hangzhou are members. This scheme of things, however, fails for T4 [34] and T5 [14].

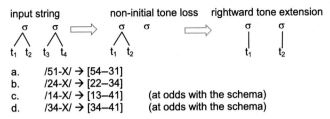

a. /51-X/ → [54–31]
b. /24-X/ → [22–34]
c. /14-X/ → [13–41] (at odds with the schema)
d. /34-X/ → [34–41] (at odds with the schema)

Figure 8 Disyllabic tone sandhi in Northern Wu Chinese (Hsieh 2008)

We shall not reproduce Hsieh's pitch tracks here, which do corroborate the sandhi descriptions in Figure 8(a-d). Notice the difference between /24-X/→ [22–34] and /14-X/→[13–41], in which X stands for the tone in the second syllable. Allowing for some phonetic under-/overshooting, /24-X/ sandhi can be justifiably said to be a case where a rising tone /lh/ splits into [l+h] for the two syllables, similar to Kukuya. Such a tale cannot be told for /14+X/, where it seems that the entire rising tone is squeezed into the first syllable and then spills over to the second, suggesting that this rising tone is not composite and cannot be split up into a sequence of tone-height features.

Given the evidence, the last word on the atomicity of tone contours has certainly not been spoken. The question of whether we continue with [high] and [low] features, include [contour] features, or displace both with a different framework altogether, must await further studies to be resolved. To the best of our knowledge, the present mainstream practice is to appeal to just [high] and [low] features in modelling tone contour.

3.4 The Complex Tone Model

In Section 2, we saw that tone is not just a matter of pitch profiles, but includes other phonetic properties. In Section 3, we saw that tone is phonologically composite. The tone's profile is not atomic, and may include register differences in addition to the tone's melodic contour. Depending on one's theoretical persuasion, the tone's melodic contour may be construed as a sequence of simple tone features like [high] and [low] so that their concatenation will yield rising, falling, dipping, or peaking profiles. If one adopts a featural system where [contour] might be a parameter, then contoured tonal melodies would be atomic. These different viewpoints will have to await research and discussion. For the moment, the simpler system would be that argued by Woo (1969) rather than that proposed in Wang (1967). The discovery of registers adds a more abstract layer of complexity. Registers are discernible only when tonal inventories are considered in their entirety so that one can see whether there are contrasting rising or falling tones that sort

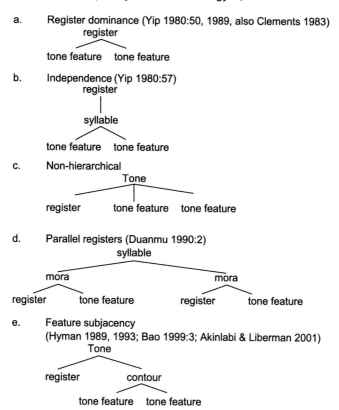

Figure 9 Relating register and contour (adapted from Yip 1995)

themselves out into different pitch ranges. With this added complexity, theorists have suggested many different models, an excellent summary of which is given in Yip (1995; see Figure 9).

It is not the place of this Element to discuss the details of the different models. The main contention between them is really just a matter of how tone register and tone features are organized. Even today, it is possible to raise arguments for or against each model, although Figure 9(e) appears to have been the most popular in studies of languages that have complex tonal inventories. With languages where the tonal inventory includes just high, low, and/or mid flat tones, the choice between the models would be much harder to make. There is, however, one property among these models that calls for attention. In Figures 9b and 9d, syllables and moras were invoked. These call to mind the issue of tone-bearing units, the subject of the next section.

4 Complexity in Manifestation

In Section 3.3, we raised the issue of tone-bearing units (TBUs), that is, the linguistic entities that bear tones. Another way of looking at it is to ask to what tones are associated, and how. Such a question arises because of our predilections in terms of what is primary and can stand alone. As an intuitive understanding, a tone must be docked on something, a syllable or word, for otherwise it might not be articulated. This intuition may coincide with the fact that the study of tone in phonology developed much later than segments and syllables. However, speakers of tone languages have often experienced situations where they have merely hummed or whistled the tone profile of a word or words in the phrase and had their interlocutors apprehend the message. In whistling and humming, there would be neither segment nor syllable, and the only perceptible features would be F0. This does not mean that one can start whistling long complex messages, as ambiguities would compound without the help of consonants and vowels. In contrast with the articulation of tone without segments, one cannot quite utter a vowel (or a syllable) without voicing, and therefore F0 – by extension, tone – is more inevitable than other vocalic or consonantal features. When thought of this way, it is easy to see tone as something that can be freely independent of other linguistic units. In any case, the questions on how tone interfaces with other linguistic units are still worth studying, whether one calls those linguistic units TBUs or not.

4.1 Tone Mobility and Stability

Experiences of whistling the tone of a word to communicate aside, phonological evidence for the independence of tone to syllables is best seen through cases where a tone appears to move from one syllable to another. This is known in the literature as 'tone mobility'; an exemplary case may be seen in Chizigula (see Figure 10) (Kenstowicz and Kisseberth 1990).

There are words in Chizigula that do not have tone, so all syllables are articulated in some kind of default pitch, presumably mid flat. Some words carry a high tone. In a basic verb such as *-lombéz-* 'ask', the high tone appears on *-béz-*. The tone, however, does not stay faithfully fixed to that syllable. Instead, with an additional suffix, the tone would keep moving rightwards and seek out the penultimate syllable. The movement works with prefixes that carry tone as well.

In the cases given for Figure 11, we can see the effect of tone mobility even more clearly. In comparing rows (a) and (b) with row (c), one can ascertain that the prefix *á-* is the source of the high tone which docks itself to the penultimate syllable of the entire morphological concatenation.

While Chizigula displaces the high tone to the penult regardless of the distance of the move, Sukuma prefers a shorter distance and would only move

a.	toneless		b.	with high tone	
i.	ku-damany-a	'to do'	i.	ku-lombéz-a	'to ask'
ii.	ku-damany-iz-a	'to do for'	ii.	ku-lombez-éz-a	'to ask for'
iii.	ku-damany-iz-an-a	'to do for each other'	iii.	ku-lombez-ez-án-a	'to ask for each other'

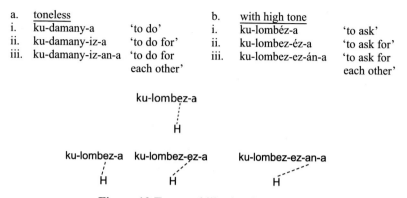

Figure 10 Tone mobility in Chizigula

Note: an animated version of the figure is available in the online resources (www.cambridge .org/wee-li).

a.	ku-	ku-gulus-a	ku-songoloz-a	ku-hugusahugus-a
		'to chase'	'to avoid'	'to shell repeatedly'
b.	ni-a-	n-a-gulus-a	n-a-songoloz-a	n-a-hugusahugus-a
		'I am chasing'	'I am avoiding'	'I shell repeatedly'
c.	á-	a-gulús-a	a-songolóz-a	a-hugusahugús-a
		'he is chasing'	'he is avoiding'	'he shells repeatedly'

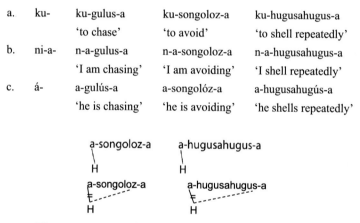

Figure 11 Adding prefixes to toneless Chizigula verbs

Note: an animated version of the figure is available in the online resources (www.cambridge .org/wee-li).

its tone two syllables to the right, illustrated in Figure 12. The underlined syllable is the 'sponsor' of the high tone.

Perhaps the most dramatic demonstration that tones are independent of syllables would come from the Cantonese diminutive suffix, as in Figure 13, which turns out to be a floating high tone; that is, a morpheme containing only a high tone without segments. Its effect can be seen when syllables that have a low or mid tone alternate to become a rising tone when in the diminutive form.

Other than the semantic evidence that this floating H is a suffix, there is also evidence from complementarity. Recall in Table 18 the traditional *Ru* tones in

a. toneless

i.	ku-sol-anij-a	'to choose simultaneously'
ii.	aka-sola ba-temi	'he chose chiefs'
iii.	ku-si-a	'to grind'

b. with H tone

i.	ku-bon-aníj-a	'to see simultaneously'
ii.	aka-bona bá-temi	'he saw chiefs'
iii.	ku-tono-lá	'to pluck'
iv.	tu-ku-sól-a	'we will choose'
v.	a-ku-ba-sol-á	'he will choose them'

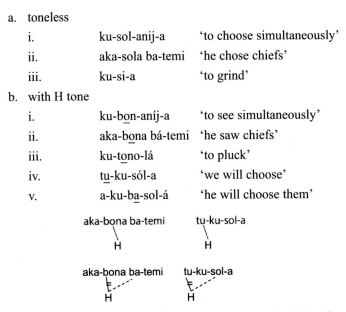

Figure 12 Sukuma (Sietsema 1989: chapter 4, also Yip 2002: 66)

Note: an animated version of the figure is available in the online resources (www.cambridge .org/wee-li).

	Citation	Diminutive	'Gloss'
a.	tsʰàn	tsʰăn	Chan
b.	jìp	jǐp	Yip
c.	kʰœ̀ŋ	kʰœ̆ŋ	Keung

Figure 13 Cantonese H tone suffix

Cantonese. All syllables closed by [p, t, k] fall under this category, so that there are no such syllables that may bear a rising or a falling tone. This is indeed so, with the exception of diminutive forms. As may be seen in Figure 13(b), [jip] would have had a low short tone as it is closed by [p]. In diminutive form, however, it may have a rising tone. Since there is no evidence (historical or otherwise) of any segmental suffix for diminutivity in Cantonese, we must concede that this is a case where a tone itself is a morpheme, floating and attaching to whatever stem becomes available, enforcing its presence even if voiceless codas would otherwise suppress it.

Table 29 Tone stability in Yoruba (Akinlabi 1985,
also Peng 2013: 347)

	Slow speech		Regular speech	
a.	rí + igbá	→	rígba	'see a calabash'
b.	rí + aʃɔ	→	ráʃɔ	'see cloth'
c.	rí + ɔbɛ̀	→	rɔ́bɛ̂	'see soup'
d.	rí + ɔ̀bɛ	→	rɔ́ˡbɛ	'see a knife'

That tone exists independently of a bearing unit can also be seen through its persistence when the host is deleted. This can be seen in Yoruba, where truncation in regular speech deletes the vowel without deleting the tone that was docked to it (see Table 29).

From the data in the table, one can see that *rí* will lose its vowel when followed by vowel-initial words in regular speech. In cases where those words begin with a toneless vowel, the high tone of *rí* can be seen to establish itself to a new host when the vowel [i] is deleted. The final case is most interesting, as it involves a clash of the tonal requirements. The word *ɔ̀bɛ* begins with a low tone, but the high tone from *rí* will compete for that vowel. Consequently, the original low tone of *ɔ̀bɛ* is displaced. However, it does not get deleted. Instead, the low tone reasserts itself as a downstep ↓. Downstep refers to the lowering of the pitch ceiling of the following syllables.

4.2 Licence to Contour

Section 4.1 has shown tone to be detachable. However, it also seems that when tones attach themselves to syllables or segments, they become constrained by what the host would license. This can be seen in the cases of *Ru* tones in Cantonese, and Hangzhou, where syllables closed by obstruent plosives do not normally license contour tones. The constraint of syllable types on tone can be seen in languages like Hausa (Table 30) and Navajo (Table 31).

The case of Hausa is quite transparent: falling tones do not appear in CV syllables, but are allowed in CVX syllables, where X stands for any segment. Navajo is similar, except that in this case, the syllable must have VV in order to license a contour tone. Prima facie, the licensing of tones is segment-dependent, so that in Hausa the requirement is to have two rime segments, and in Navajo two vowels. If we go by the model that contour tones are concatenated from simple tone features [high] and [low], then it appears that these features may attach only to certain segments as specified by the language. Such a view predicts that syllables can bear very complex tones such as double-peaking or double-dipping tones if there are enough segments. This prediction has not been borne out across all known

Table 30 Tones in Hausa (Gordon 2006: 295 and Zec 2011)

	Low	High	Falling
CV	fàsáá	sáfúú 'row, line'	-
CVV	mà*à*máá 'breast'	ráánáá 'sun'	láàláá 'indolence'
CVN	ràndáá	mándáá	máǹtáá 'forgot'
	'large water pot'	'dark Bornu medicinal salt'	
CVO	fàskíí	máskóó	râssáá
	'being very broad'	'large blacksmith's hammer'	'branches'

Table 31 Tones in Navajo (Zhang 2002: 52, citing Wall and Morgan 1958; Young and Morgan 1987; and Hoijer 1945)

	High	Low	Falling	Rising
CV	sání 'old one'	ṇʧà 'you're crying'	-	-
CVN	háá?ált'è? 'exhumation'	pìkʰìn 'his house'	-	-
CVO	tìníʃ?ìì? 'I'm looking'	pìtɨ 'his blood'	-	-
CVV	túú 'this'	ɬìkàì 'white'	sáànìì 'old woman'	hákòónèè? 'let's go'
CVVN	àstáán 'woman'	pìjììn 'his song'	tàtíníìl?ììɬ 'we'll look at him'	tèíl?á 'they extend'
CVVO	ɬóó? 'fish'	pìnìì? 'his face'	tʰáà?tì 'three times'	tèíʒníílton 'they shot at him'

Legend: C: consonant, V: vowel, N: nasal/sonorant, O: obstruent

human languages. Instead, tone complexity appears to be predicated only on a heavy and light two-way distinction of syllable weight: heavy syllables may bear complex tones, maximally to three tonal features, whereas light syllables may normally only bear level tones. This suggests the mora.

In a moraic conception, syllables are either heavy (bimoraic) or light (mono-moraic), although in rare cases such as Hindi, superheavy syllables (trimoraic) have been observed. Ignoring trimoraicity for the moment, Hausa's patterns can be adopted to a moraic treatment: CV syllables, being monomoraic, may bear only one tone feature, whereas CVX types are bimoraic and bear two different features. Such a conception would allow each mora to be associated with a single tone feature. As for Navajo, one will have to hypothesize that only vowels are moraic.

A particularly complex case for the mora as a TBU can be seen in Thai, where both moraicity and segmental properties come into play. The tonal inventory given in Table 32 below offers phonological abstractions of Thai, so actual phonetic forms may differ from them.

There are a few things that are puzzling about the gaps in Table 32. It appears inexplicable that CVVO should not allow mid, high, or rising tones if CVV syllables may take any of the tones. (Although it should be noted that of the more than ninety Tai languages, of which Thai is one, many do allow CVVO syllables to have rising tones, see for instance Saeng-gnam 2006, cited in Dockum 2019.) However, these gaps have been attributed to diachronic explanations (see Gedney (1972), Pittayaporn (2009), Dockum (2019)). Modern speakers, without access to history, must find a synchronic account for this as a grammatical pattern. More unexpected is how CVO syllables may have high tones when CVVO may not.

Morén and Zsiga (2006) noted that obstruents' codas in Thai are always accompanied by glottalization, a feature that impedes vocal fold vibration, and may reasonably be regarded as entailing a [low] tone. This [low] tone, however, is unable to manifest itself on the obstruent coda because in Thai, such codas are voiceless. The low tone therefore finds expression only by association to the preceding vowel. Assuming the mid tone to be a case of phonological tonelessness, Morén and Zsiga could attribute the absence of mid tones for CVO and CVVO syllables to the presence of a [low] tone feature on O. The [low] tone of O would mask falling tones because even if the V takes a [high] tone, O's [low] would find itself without a V host and must remain silent with the voiceless O.

As for the absence of rising tone, the V would be required to start with [low], but [high] cannot be associated with O, which already comes with its own [low]. With no [high] tone feature, there can be no rising tone. Although the CVO gaps can be accounted for this way, the CVVO tone gaps remain unaccounted for.

With two Vs in CVVO, any assumption that tones are associated with segments will be unable to explain the tone gaps, since there are now adequate vowels for both [low] and [high] tone features. Morén and Zsiga's analysis is that Thai syllables are bimoraic, and that the mora is the TBU, not the segments. With only two moras, CVO and CVVO would have the same number of positions for hosting tone features. Once the second mora is associated with [low] through the endowment of the glottalized O, any tonal profile forbidden by CVO would apply similarly to CVVO, as schematically presented in Figure 14.

Table 32 Thai tones and syllable types (Morén and Zsiga 2006; also Gandour 1974 and 1977)

syllable \ tone	Mid	Low	High	Falling	Rising
CVV	naa 'rice field'	nàà 'custard apple'	náá 'aunt'	nââ 'face'	nǎǎ 'thick'
CVN	laŋ 'crate'	làŋ 'to flow'	lám 'to go beyond'	lâm 'sturdy'	lǎŋ 'back'
CVVN	laaŋ 'omen'	ŋàaŋ 'chime'	láaŋ 'to wash'	lâaŋ 'below'	lǎaŋ 'grandchild'
CVO	-	làk 'stake'	lák 'to steal'	-	-
CVVO	-	làak 'various'	-	lâak 'to tow'	-

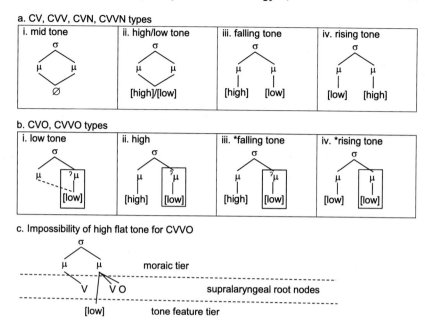

Figure 14 Moraic representation of Thai tones constraints from glottalized obstruents

In Figure 14(a), both moras are free to associate with any tone, or even be toneless. In Figure 14(b), the second mora is associated with O, indicated here with a superscript [?], and thus necessarily bears a [low] tone. As long as [low] is associated to this mora, it would be invisible, indicated by the box, as the voiceless obstruent would prevent its manifestation. From Figure 14(b), it should be evident why mid-level, falling, and rising tones are impossible for CVO and CVVO syllables in Thai. As to why CVVO is incompatible with high-level tones, the explanation is to be found in the fact that the second mora would associate with the second V, and thus the [low] tone from O would always find manifestation (but see also Haudricourt (1954) and Gedney (1972) for a diachronic account). This is illustrated in Figure 14(c). The [low] associated with the second mora was entailed by the glottalized O. However, with the second V also associated, that V would serve as the carrier of [low], rendering it impossible for Thai CVVO syllables to be a high flat tone. It should be noted that the high flat tone in Thai varies according to whether it is in the loan or native stratum. We are unable to discuss this here, but see Perkins (2013).

Together with the examples of Hausa and Navajo, Thai shows that the best case may be made for the mora to be the TBU, and it is to the mora that tones are docked. It is having two moras available that would license contour tones, although, as seen in Thai, additional constraints may come from segments that thwart the manifestation of tone features. This position allows the greatest coverage of facts. Even in languages such as Chinese, where traditionally syllables are thought to be TBUs, evidence from toneless elements would lead to analyses in favour of the mora.

4.3 Tonelessness and Tone-Bearing Units

The preceding sections have witnessed a few examples of tonelessness. In Thai, that is the assumed situation for syllables with mid flat tones. They are reasonably considered toneless because phonetically, the mid tone is easiest to produce, and thus least marked. However, more importantly, it is also because there is no definite movement towards a target, which implies phonological specification of its tonelessness. Further, that assumption provides part of the explanation as to why the mid flat tone is never found with CVO and CVVO syllables. In the treatment of Wu (cf. Figure 8 in Section 3.3), we see that syllables can have their tones deleted and then inherit the tones of other syllables through spreading. In Kukuya and Mende, syllables begin their lives toneless, only to receive the tones as the word tone spreads across that domain (cf. Section 3.3). Returning to the issue of TBUs, if contours are licensed by moras, then loss of moras would similarly reduce the tone features of a syllable. This is easily seen in Mandarin Chinese languages, of which Standard Chinese – artificially constructed for various political reasons in the first half of the twentieth century, but fundamentally based on the Beijing dialect – may serve as our first example (Table 33).

Table 33 illustrates that, in a disyllabic word such as ma_{55} *ma* 'mother', the preceding syllable has a lexical tone, for example [55], while the second syllable is phonologically toneless, either base-generated or rendered so by morphological processes. For the toneless syllables, Table 33 provides the tonal realization of the toneless syllables in terms of low or high, as the pitch

Table 33 Pitch of toneless syllables in Standard Chinese
(see Wang 2002, among others)

Tonal values of preceding syllable	Tonal realization of toneless syllable	Examples
Tone 1 [55]	Low	ma_{55} *ma* 'mother', $dong_{55}$*xi* 'stuff'
Tone 2 [35]	Low	$niang_{35}$*niang* 'ladyship', pan_{35} *zi* 'plate'
Tone 3 [214] / [21]	High	nai_{21} *nai* 'grandmother', yi_{21} *zi* 'chair'
Tone 4 [51]	Low	di_{51} *di* 'younger brother', yao_{51} *shi* 'key'

height is not indicative of tone and the absolute height is not important. The point is that these toneless syllables never carry a full tone. Phonetic studies by Lin and Yan (1980) reveal that these toneless syllables are about half the length of Tone 4, which is the shortest in the inventory of Standard Chinese tones. Wang (2002) interprets this to be due to there being only one mora in these toneless syllables. In his telling, monomoraicity licenses only singular tone features, the default of which is presumably [low]. Tone 3 assigns a [high] to the toneless syllable because it is underlyingly dipping and has three features associated with two moras of the syllable bearing that tone. With a toneless monomoraic appendage, that final [high] feature can be relegated. The case of Standard Chinese tonelessness must involve loss of moraicity. This loss is not predicated on loss of rhyme segments, as may be seen in the examples for $nai_{21}nai$ 'grandmother', and $niang_{35}niang$ 'ladyship'. This corroborates the view presented for Thai, where segments and tones are on different planes, even if both associate to the mora.

Typologically, one would expect there to be a language where tonelessness is due only to the loss of tone features while preserving the moras. Indeed this is the case with Urumqi Mandarin. Wang (2002) reports that in this language, the toneless syllables are not shorter in length, and do in fact carry a more stable pitch contour, albeit neutralized (see Table 34).

In the Urumqi examples (ai, bi, and ci), the monosyllabic forms show the tones of these morphemes in their citation forms. In contexts where they are neutralized, say when lexicalized, their tones change largely following the pattern given in Figure 15 below.

In Urumqi Mandarin, the tones of σ_2 are dissociated and erased, leaving two empty moras. The nearest tone feature from the preceding syllable σ_1 spreads to

Table 34 Urumqi neutral tones (Wei 2001: 25)

a.	i.	$tian_{44}$ 'sky'
	ii.	jin_{44} **$tian_{51}$** 'now sky (today)'
	iii.	$ming_{44}$ **$tian_{31}$** 'bright sky (tomorrow)'
	iv.	xia_{21} **$tian_{13}$** 'summer sky (summer)'
b.	i.	$yang_{51}$ 'sun'
	ii.	tai_{21} **$yang_{13}$** 'the sun'
c.	i.	li_{51} 'reason'
	ii.	dao_{21} **li_{13}** 'way and reason (principle)'
d.	i.	$liang_{213}$ 'bright'
	ii.	yue_{21} **$liang_{13}$** 'moon'
	iii.	$zhao_{13}$ $liang_{213}$ 'make bright' (Wei 2001: 38)

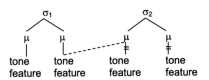

Figure 15 Tonelessness in Urumqi Mandarin

the first mora of σ_2. The second mora remains untouched and surfaces as mid. This would explain why the toneless syllable is rising when the preceding syllable ends low, and falling when the preceding syllable ends high. Crucially, the moras of the toneless syllables remained, hence the unshortened length as noted by Wang (2002). Herein lies the difference in how tonelessness works in Urumqi Mandarin and Standard Chinese.

This section shows that tone, which has been considered suprasegmental (i.e., beyond the segment), is in fact autosegmental (i.e., independent of its host). While associated with TBUs, a tone does have the ability to detach itself from these hosts and to find itself new ones or to be deleted. The independence of tone makes it unsurprising that tone should exhibit alternation patterns on their own, independent of their bearing units. This is the subject of the next section on tone sandhi.

5 Complexity in Triggering Tone Sandhi

Section 4 established what is known as the autosegmentality of tone, that is, tone's existence on a plane separate from its hosts such as moras, syllables, or segments. With this qualification, we now move on to look at how tones interact with each other. In many instances, sorting out what triggers the patterns can itself be a major challenge. Consider, for instance, the following sandhi patterns in Tianjin, which has four tones in its inventory.

In Table 35, the tones of the Tianjin inventory are given in the first row and column. With four tones, there will be sixteen logical ditonal combinations, six of which trigger sandhi, and the remaining ten (in grey cells) do not (Wee, Yan, and Chen 2005, but see Zhang and Liu 2011 for the most recent phonetically accurate study, and Ma and Jia 2006 for a different view).

5.1 Contour Principles: Tianjin and Hakha Lai

As remarked earlier, a tonological account of Tianjin began with Li and Liu's (1985) report. Yip (1989) was probably the first to discern that the patterns are instantiations of the Obligatory Contour Principle (Leben 1973 and Goldsmith 1976), which we may define as follows.

Obligatory Contour Principle (OCP)
Adjacent tones must not be identical.

Table 35 Rudimentary tone sandhi patterns in Tianjin

1st σ \ 2nd σ	T1: L(ow)	T2: H(igh)	T3: R(ising)	T4: F(alling)
T(one) 1: L	L	▨	▨	▨
T2: H	▨			
T3: R		L+H	H+R	L+F
T4: F	L	▨	▨	L+F

The way the OCP is stated here is deliberately vague, but it should be clear how it applies to L+L, R+R, and F+F, all of which are collocations of identical tones and undergo tone sandhi in Tianjin. As for F→H/__L, the pattern becomes obvious when one breaks F down into its constituent features [high][low]+[low]→[high]+[low]. In this case, it is the removal of an offending [low] tone feature to prevent adjacency of identical tone elements. The observation applies to the latter-discovered additional patterns R→L/__ {F, H} as well, since that would be [low][high]+[high]([low]) where there is an adjacency of [high]. Yip's (1989) insight is that the OCP must be allowed to apply at two different levels: the level of the tone contour as a constituent, and the level of the tone feature. Although the OCP may be used as the impetus for all the sandhi-triggering collocations, it leaves unexplained why H+H and F+R do not trigger tone sandhi (but see Wee 2015 for an attempt through prosody).

Hyman (2007) suggests a radically different approach, using an antithetical NoCP to match the OCP.

No Contour Principle (NoCP, Hyman 1978, 2007)
Minimize the ups and downs in pitch contours.

In Hyman's telling, the reason R+R and F+F trigger sandhi is because these are rollercoaster situations, respectively [low][high].[low][high] and [high] [low].[high][low]. Removal of a feature from the first tone contour would reduce the number of ups and downs. Hyman's approach has a few attractive features. Firstly, there is thus no sandhi-triggering impetus for H+H. Secondly, the approach can be grounded phonetically on the pressure for ease of articulation. However, there are a number of difficulties as well. Some reason would have to be concocted for L+L, F+L, and R+H/F to undergo sandhi. Also, one needs to explain why R+R should not surface as L+R and F+F should not surface as H+F. These options would have even fewer ups and downs while removing also only just one tone feature from the first tone.

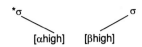

Figure 16 Intersyllabic No Contour Principle (NoCP)

Hyman's NoCP may not fit very naturally with Tianjin, but it works beautifully in Hakha Lai, which has an inventory of three tones: falling, rising, and low. Of nine ($=3^2$) ditonal collocations, four trigger tone sandhi. These are presented in Table 36.

In Table 36, the grey cells are those where the tonal collocations do not trigger tone sandhi. If we break the tones down into [high] and [low] tone features, a pattern quickly emerges. Across syllables, tones must agree in their tone features. Those that do not – FF, RR, RL, and LF – will undergo tone sandhi either by removing the offending tone feature from the second syllable (e.g., F→L/F__ and F→L/L__) or the first (e.g., R→L/L__), or by metathesis of the two tone features in the second syllable (R→F/R__). In essence, the No Contour Principle (NoCP) can be pictorially represented as in Figure 16.

Going back to Tianjin, it is possible that neither the OCP nor the NoCP applies there. In Zhang and Liu's (2011) very rigorously constructed phonetic study, the authors obtained F0 profiles from twelve speakers, which they time-normalized and averaged to examine whether Tianjin tone sandhi happens as described in Table 35. Their findings are summarized in the following list.

Zhang and Liu's (2011) findings on Tianjin tone sandhi

a. T(one)1 neutralizes to T2, not T3, if followed by another T1
b. T4 before T4 does not undergo sandhi, hence may be obsolete among the tested speakers
c. T3 undergoes sandhi to be somewhat like T2 before T3, but does not neutralize with T2
d. T3 undergoes sandhi to be somewhat like T1 before T2 and T4, but does not neutralize with T1
e. T4 undergoes sandhi to be somewhat like T2 before T1, but does not neutralize with T2

Note that Zhang and Liu (2011) dispreferred the descriptions L, H, R, and F for the four Tianjin tones, and had refrained from committing to the idea that sandhi in Tianjin is category-changing. Their reservations can be understood in part from how descriptions of Tianjin tones had undergone some abstractions from the earliest fieldwork to acoustic analyses to phonological features, roughly reflected in Table 37.

Table 36 Hakha Lai tone inventory and ditonal sandhi (Hyman and VanBik, 2004)

1st σ \ 2nd σ	F(alling)	R(ising)	L(ow)
F	FL̲(=hl.l)	FR(=hl.lh)	FL(=hl.l)
R	RF(=lh.hl)	RF̲(=lh.hl)	L̲L(=l.l)
L	L̲L̲(=l.l)	LR(=l.lh)	L̲.L̲(=l.l)

Examples

Tone	F(alling)	R(ising)	L(ow)
F(alling)	ka hmàà 'my wound'	ka lûŋ 'my heart'	ka tlâàŋ 'my mountain'
	ka zùù 'my beer'	ka làw 'my field'	ka ráal 'my enemy'
R(ising)	ka kèé 'my leg'	ka hrôm 'my throat'	ka kôóy 'my friend'
	ka ʔòó 'my voice'	ka tsâl 'my foreheard'	ka tsáán 'my time'
L(low)	ka sàà 'my animal'	ka ràŋ 'my horse'	ka kôòm 'my corn'
	ka hnìì 'my skirt'	ka kàl 'my kidney'	ka bòòr 'my bunch'

Table 37 Tone inventory of Tianjin (adapted from Shi 1987 with augmentation)

	Tone 1	Tone 2	Tone 3	Tone 4
Luo (1956)	[11]	[55]	[24]	[42]
Li and Liu (1983)	[21]	[34]	[213]	[53]
Guo (1982)	[21]	[45]	[213]	[53]
Davison (1982)	[21, 11]	[45]	[24]	[53]
Li and Liu (1985)	[21]	[45]	[213]	[53]
Shi (1987)	[21]	[45]	[13]	[53]
Chen (2000), Wang (2002)	L(ow)	H(igh)	R(ising)	F(alling)

Figure 17 Tianjin tones (reconstructed from Chao 1922)

We cannot resist sharing a rather accurate impressionistic depiction from Chao (1922). Chao's musical transcription was obtained by mimicking the tones of Tianjin with the Qin (also called Guqin) (see Figure 17), a plucked string musical instrument that is almost sacred to the traditional Chinese literati. The Qin has a flat fingerboard that allows sliding of the left-hand fingers, similar to a violin.

Zhang and Liu's attention to phonetic accuracies is laudable, although one should remember that Tianjin is not a language that makes a five-way distinction on tone heights, so a ±1 difference in tone value is really inconsequential. Comparing Li and Liu (1983) and Li and Liu (1985), for example, it can be noticed that even the same authors notated the tones slightly differently within just two years. It is the same attention to phonetic accuracies that Zhang and Liu highlighted in saying that the result of sandhi produces only tones somewhat like the extant tone categories. Zhang and Liu may have demonstrated that sandhied tones may not have neutralized acoustically, although perceptory discernment has not been tested. Phonologically, however, derived forms and underived forms may be different. In any case, Zhang and Liu's (2011) cue may allow us to sidestep the debates of an OCP or NoCP solution, but we are left without any deeper explanation to the Tianjin patterns. On such a basis, Zhang and Liu (2016) called to question whether and how the Tianjin patterns are productive; they found that speakers may overapply or underapply the sandhi rules to phonotactically well-formed nonce words, as is true of the productivity of many other patterns in different languages. The productivity of a tone sandhi rule may be influenced by frequency effects as well as the nature of the rule, for example, being phonologically opaque or not. Opaque rules either fail to apply in triggering environments or they apply to non-surfacing intermediate phonological forms, and these might conceivably be more cognitively demanding. Similar conclusions were reached by Yan and Zhang (2016) for Wuxi, and by Zhang and Lai (2008) and Zhang, Lai, and Sailor (2011) for Taiwanese Min. It is to the Taiwanese story that we now turn. In the Taiwanese story, Chuang, Chang, and Hsieh (2011) offer an ingenious rebuttal, which will come towards the end of Section 5.2.

5.2 Contrast Preservation: Taiwanese Tone Circle

In the preceding section of Tianjin, the astute reader would notice an interesting phenomenon that appears to be a chain shift. There, in one particular chain, the F tone undergoes sandhi to L, the L tone to R, and R to H. Another chain would be the R undergoing sandhi to L, and L back to R. This is shown pictorially in Figure 18.

In the case of Tianjin, the choice of which sandhi rule to apply depends on what the following tone is. The case of Taiwanese is different and much more complicated, as diagrammatically shown in Figure 19.

Again setting aside the tones of syllables closed by obstruent codas, Taiwanese Min syllables may bear any of the six tones shown in Figure 19. However, each of these tones will alternate to some other tone when followed by another syllable, as shown in the examples with the syllable *si*. Sandhi is not conditioned by the tone of the following syllable. An account for Taiwanese

Figure 18 Targets of sandhi in Tianjin

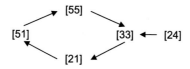

si$_{55}$ 'poetry'	**si**$_{33}$ bun$_{24}$ 'poetry and prose'
si$_{33}$ 'temple'	**si**$_{21}$ tsiŋ$_{55}$ 'temple monk'
si$_{21}$ 'four'	**si**$_{51}$ tiam$_{51}$ 'four o'clock'
si$_{51}$ 'die'	**si**$_{55}$ laŋ$_{24}$ 'dead people'
si$_{24}$ 'time'	**si**$_{33}$ kan$_{55}$ 'time span; time'

Figure 19 Tone sandhi circle in Taiwanese

tone sandhi would require explications of why any non-final syllable must undergo alternation (i.e., explanation of the sandhi site) and on how the resultant tones are arrived at (i.e., explanation of the sandhi target).

That the sandhi targets form a chain – a circular one in fact – makes any treatment based entirely on markedness implausible. This is because a markedness trigger on any given tone would lead ultimately to an unmarked (or least marked) form and the chain would stop, and no circularity would result. In fact, one could have jumped directly to the least marked form and have no chains at all. Further, markedness cannot have been due in any part to the following tone since every tone undergoes sandhi regardless of which tone follows it. We shall leave this issue unaddressed for the moment.

Although the inventory of Taiwanese tones does not suggest a clear register bifurcation, a pattern emerges if register is postulated as shown in Figure 20.

In Figure 20, we follow Hsiao's (2015) notation of using Hr to mean Higher register, and Lr to mean Lower register. The lowercase letters [h] and [l] are tone features. The pattern in Figure 20 is that as one moves from each station to the next along the tone circle, either the tone register or the tone contour alternates, but never both. If one starts with [24], which is [Lr,lh], that tone undergoes sandhi to become [Lr,h]. This preserves the register, but flattens the tone contour. From [Lr,h] to [Lr,hl], the register is also preserved, but this time the tone is made to contour. From [Lr,hl] to [Hr,hl], however, the register is now changed, but the contour is preserved. The next step in the chain preserves the register again, and flattens the contour to [Hr,h]. Finally, the register alternates to [Lr,h] without a change in contour. If one looks only at the circle, excluding [Lr,lh], it looks as if register and tone contour take turns to alternate.

Having found a handle for grappling with Taiwanese tone sandhi through the complexity of its tone structure, an account for it would require a cocktail of rather sophisticated tools. For the tools, we now turn to the theoretical framework of Optimality Theory (OT, Prince and Smolensky 1993/2004, among others), which accommodates different mechanisms including markedness, contrast preservation, faithfulness, and a postulation on historical developments. To see how these work, here are a list of constraints.

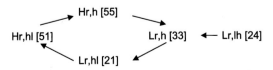

Figure 20 Taiwanese tone sandhi circle in terms of register and contour

Constraints at work in Taiwanese Tone Sandhi

*Non-FinCtr
Do not allow contour melodies in non-final positions.

PC (Preservation of Contrast, see Łubowicz 2003, 2012 for original insight)
Do not be identical to the output of a different input in the same morpho-phonological environment.

Ident[ctr]
The output tone contour must be identical with the corresponding input tone contour.

Ident[Rg]
The output tone register must be identical with the corresponding input tone register.

We begin with *Non-FinCtr, a markedness constraint which would apply to three of the five Taiwanese tones (i.e., Hr,hl, Lr, hl and Lr, lh) when they are in non-final positions. Using an optimality theoretic framework, one can see it at work in the tableau in Table 38.

Following OT conventions, candidates for a given input are listed along the first column. Along the top row, constraints are given in order of priority, where dashed separators indicate the lack of ranking arguments between two adjacent constraints. For every candidate, each violation of a constraint is indicated with *. From these one may assess when a candidate would be eliminated as inferior

Table 38 Markedness as a trigger

a. input: Hr,hl##	*Non-FinCtr	Ident[ctr]	Ident[Rg]
i. Hr,h		*!	
☞ ii. Hr,hl			
iii. Lr,h		*!	*
iv. Lr,hl			*!
b. input: Hr,hl+... cf. Hr,hl→Hr,hl			
☞ i. Hr,h + ...		*	
ii. Hr,hl + ...	*!		
iii. Lr,h + ...		*	*!
iv. Lr,hl + ...	*!		*

Legend: * violation marks ! critical violation ☞ optimal candidate/actual output to its competitors. Eventually, a candidate would be optimal (not perfect, but the best under the constraint ranking) and hence predicted as the output.

IDENT[ctr] and IDENT[Rg] are faithfulness constraints that require output candidates to be identical to the inputs. In other words, they militate against alternation, although they can be overridden by constraints that outrank them. In Table 38(a), these constraints preserve the falling tone contour of the input. However, in Table 38(b), *Non-FinCtr outranks them, and flattens the non-final falling tone. Although a similar analysis can be made for the other two contour tones, Wee (2019: 174–82 and 2020) suggests that Hr,hl→[Hr,h] had been seminal (although see Thomas (2008) for a story that begins with Lr,lh→[Lr,h]).

With Table 38 in place, /Hr,h/ would find itself in trouble if PC were dominant, as may be seen in Table 39.

The insight that PC is relevant in Taiwanese tone sandhi comes from Barrie (2006), who first applied it to a very closely related language, Xiamen (also known as Amoy). Starting with Table 39(a), the problem

Table 39 Chain reactions with PC

a. input: Hr,h+... cf. Hr,hl→Hr,h	PC	*NON-FINCTR	IDENT[ctr]	IDENT[Rg]
i. Hr,h + ...	*/Hr,hl/!			
ii. Hr,hl + ...		*!	*	
☞ iii. Lr,h + ...				*
iv. Lr,hl + ...		*!		*
b. input: Lr,h+... cf. /Hr,h/→[Lr,h]				
i. Lr,h	*/Hr,h/!			
☞ ii. Lr,hl		*	*	
iii. Hr,h	*/Hr,hl/!			*
iv. Hr,hl		*	*	*!
c. input: Lr,hl+... cf./Lr,h/ → Lr,hl				
i. Lr,h	*/Hr,h/!		*	
ii. Lr,hl	*/Lr,h/!	*		
iii. Hr,h	*/Hr,hl/!		*	*
☞ iv. Hr,hl		*	*	*

Table 40 Deriving /Lr,lh/ → [Lr,h]

*NON-FINR

Do not have non-final rising tones.

input: Lr,lh+...	*NON-FINR	PC	*NON-FINCTR	IDENT [ctr]	IDENT [Rg]
i. Hr,h + ...		*/Hr,hl/		*	*!
ii. Hr,hl + ...		*/Lr,hl/	*!	*	*
☞ iii. Lr,h + ...		*/Hr,h/		*	
iv. Lr,hl + ...		*/Lr,h/	*!	*	
v. Lr,lh + ...	*!		*		

here is that /Hr,h/ can no longer surface unchanged if the surface form in the non-final position is not to be neutralized with the output of /Hr,hl/. Recall that /Hr,hl/→[Hr,h] is due to *NON-FINCTR (Table 38). The next best choice is to change register to get [Lr,h] as its output. This moves the onus of contrast preservation to /Lr,h/ which now may not surface unchanged. In Table 39(b), we can see how that would, curiously, yield a contour tone, in violation of *NON-FINCTR. The reason for tolerating such a violation is because the other flat tones of the Hr register are already taken. The same reasoning applies to /Lr,hl/ to yield [Hr,hl] as shown in Table 39(c). At this point, we now have captured the core circle given in Figure 20. To get /Lr,lh/→[Lr,h], Wee (2019, 2020) postulates one final overriding markedness constraint, presented in Table 40.

The analysis presented here predicts that historically, /Hr,hl/→[Hr,l] must have happened before the others. To the best of our knowledge, there has been no documentation yet discovered to support or refute this claim. Suffice for now to say that Taiwanese presents a rather complicated phenomenon that speaks to the complexity of tone.

Zhang and Liu's (2016) experimental study provided empirical grounds for querying the reality of Tianjin tone sandhi as part of the phonological grammar. Nearly a decade before that, the complexity of Taiwanese tone sandhi caught the attention of Zhang and Lai (2008), who showed that speakers were largely unable to apply the sandhi patterns to phonotactically valid non-word Taiwanese syllables. Despite this convincing study, Chuang, Chang, and Hsieh (2011) provided strong grounds for reconsideration through an experiment on back-formation. Using mono-morphemic dissyllabic sequences and Japanese loanwords, Chuang, Chang, and Hsieh created semantically opaque stimuli of ditonal Taiwanese sequences which they presented to their subjects. The subjects were to articulate each constituent tone in isolation. If indeed tone sandhi were unproductive, then each isolated tone would be returned as identical to the form in the ditonal stimulus. However, the subjects produced each isolated tone different from its form in the given stimulus string, but corresponding, to various degrees, to what would have been the pre-sandhied form. Chuang *et al.* inferred that the sandhi rules must be part of the phonological grammar.

Debates such as these in tonological studies are not a matter of who got it wrong. Both are rigorously executed empirical studies. One should instead look for a resolution through covering both apparently contradictory sets of facts. In this case, it may be something like how Zhang and Lai's non-word stimuli were not completely assimilated by their subjects at the time of the experiment, and were treated as foreign in their attempt at articulation. As for Chuang *et al.*'s experiment, the task was retrieval and the subjects would have treated the stimuli as Taiwanese articulations, albeit non-words. Such experiments attest to the phonological reality of tone sandhi as part of the mental grammar of the speakers.

5.3 Incoherent Triggers: Longyan Min and Changting Hakka

Although challenging, Tianjin and Taiwanese present tone sandhi for which analysts have found coherent stories. Tianjin patterns may be construed as largely the result of the OCP applying at the level of the tone contour or the tone features. Taiwanese patterns may be analysed in terms of contrast preservation in response to neutralizing forces of markedness constraints. There are, however, many cases that remain elusive. We present two such cases here as an invitation to all who like a challenge, and also in the spirit of transparency as concerns what remains dark in the field.

5.3.1 Longyan Min

Longyan Min had not caught the attention of fieldwork linguists until recently. Yan and Luo (2008) reported that it has six basic monosyllable tones whose values are /35/, /21/, /31/, /24/, /55/, and /51/. A cursory scan may suggest the relevance of tone register since there are two rising tones /35/ and /24/. If one treats /51/ and /31/ as falling tones from two different registers, then a symmetry in the tone inventory is quite possible, as suggested in Table 41.

Table 41 Longyan Min tone inventory

	Rising	Falling	Level
H(igh) r(egister)	/35/	/51/	/55/
Lr	/24/	/31/	/21/

Table 42 Ditonal sandhi patterns in Longyan

2nd σ 〳 1st σ	/Hr,lh/ /35/	/Lr,lh/ /24/	/Hr,hl/ /51/	/Lr,hl/ /31/	/Hr,h/ /55/	/Lr,l/ /21/
/Hr,lh/ /35/	[33+35]	[33+24]	[33+51]	[35+31]	[33+55]	[35+21]
/Lr,lh/ /24/	[31+35]	[31+24]	[31+51]	[24+31]	[31+55]	[24+21]
/Hr,hl/ /51/	[33+35]	[33+24]	[33+51]	[33+31]	[33+55]	[21+21]
/Lr,hl/ /31/	[31+35]	[31+24]	[31+51]	[24+31]	[31+55]	[24+21]
/Hr,h/ /55/	[33+35]	[33+24]	[33+51]	[55+31]	[33+55]	[55+21]
/Lr,l/ /21/	[33+35]	[33+24]	[33+51]	[33+31]	[33+55]	[21+21]

Of the thirty-six ditonal combinations ($=6^2$), only eleven do not trigger tone sandhi (indicated as greyed cells in Table 42).

In all cases, the site of tone sandhi is always on the first syllable, and the second remains unchanged. The target tones of sandhi (i.e., tones derived from sandhi) are few: only [33], [35], [24], and [21]. Of these, [33] is not part of the tone inventory given in Table 41. Since it is a mid flat tone, one may postulate it to be toneless default.

To find a coherent story for Longyan Min, one may look at (i) the possibility of triggers in the tonal collocation, (ii) the relevance of the first tone in determining the output, and (iii) the relevance of the second tone in determining the output. One can rule out contrast preservation for Longyan Min since neutralization is evidently massive, as seen in Table 42.

Starting with the possibility of triggers in the tonal collocation, let us consider the OCP. There are grounds of the OCP's being active in Longyan Min given that there are no surface collocations of rising tones (cf. first two rows and first two columns of Table 42). With respect to falling tones, this is still true for /Lr.hl/ in the fourth column, but not for /Hr,hl/ in the third column. However, hope of applying the OCP is dashed by the fact that there are OCP-offending inputs that do not trigger sandhi (e.g., [21+21] and [51+31]). There are also sandhi cases that do not violate OCP (e.g., /24/→[31]/__ [55] and /51/→[33]/__[24]. Both cases have different registers and contours. Also see /24/→[31]/__[35], although adjacent tone features are different). Further, surface forms may potentially be OCP-violating (e.g., [31+51], which have similar contours, [24+31], which have the same registers, and [21+21], which has two identical tones). Moving on to consider the NoCP. If we leniently allow [3] to be ambiguous between [Lr,h] and [IIr, l], then [33]-initial sequences can be said to flow naturally into any following tone that begins with [2, 3], or even [5]. However, how could the NoCP explain /24/→[31]/__[51/55] and /55/→[33]/__[55]? One would also need to explain why NoCP had not required /31+55/ to undergo sandhi. Neither the OCP nor the NoCP offers a ready answer to Longyan Min triggers. The authors are stuck on this one, but let us see if we have better luck with the relevance of the first tone in determining the output.

As far as we can tell from Table 42, all input Lr-initial tones preserve their registers on the surface. Thus, /24/ in the second row and /31/ in the fourth row both may surface as either [31] or [24]. Also, /21/ in the sixth row surfaces as either [33] or [21], granting ambiguity in the interpretation of [33]. Preservation of register would have applied to Hr-initial tones as well, with the singular exception of /51/→[21]/__[21] (third row, final column). As for the contour shapes of the initial tone, there appears to be no consistency in how given input contours may surface, which leads us to look at whether the second tone might have an impact on the initial tones. However, here we find little hope. There is no consistency in the register between the outputs of the two tones. The first tone surfaces in registers that may or may not agree with the second, so the second tone does not supply tone register (regardless of agreement or polarity) in the sandhi process. There is also no clear consistency in the tone contour or the adjacency of tone features that would suggest the second tone is at work in determining the output of the initial tone.

Yan and Luo (2008) were among the first to do fieldwork on Longyan. In that same year, Yan shared their results with Wee (one of the two authors of this Element), enquiring as to whether a phonological account might be possible. Unable to make much headway, Wee asked Yan for the original recordings, and was satisfied that the transcriptions were quite accurate. Without a coherent

Table 43 Changting Hakka tone patterns (Chen, Yan, and Wee 2004)

a. Tone inventory

Tone	Level	Rising	Falling
High	H 55		
Mid	M 33	R 24	F 42
Low	L 21		

b. Ditonal sandhi patterns

1st σ \ 2nd σ	H	M	L	R	F
H	H+H	F+M	F+L	F+R	H+F
M	M+H	M+M	L+L	L+R	M+F
L	M+H	M+M	L+L	L+R	M+F
R	R+H	H+M	R+F	R+R	M+R
F	L+H	R+M	R+F	L+R	M+F

analysis, the theoretical significance of the Longyan tone data will have to remain hidden.

5.3.2 Changting Hakka

Changting Hakka offers another complex case of tonal phonology that has remained enigmatic since it was first reported in Chen, Yan, and Wee (2004), and then in Chen, Wee, and Yan (2008) in a summarized form. Changting Hakka has five monosyllabic tones. Table 43(a) provides the tonal inventory, and Table 43(b) the patterns of ditonal concatenation. As before, collocations that do not trigger sandhi are in grey cells.

From Table 43(a), there does not seem to be any motivation for distinctions in register, so we shall not postulate that, although the possibility remains open. The inventory looks straightforward enough and rather symmetrical, with the exception of the M tone, whose status might be ambivalent. In Changting Hakka, postulating M as a toneless default would require an explanation of why all other tones alternate when preceding it. With respect to M, there is also a tone circle, H→F/__M, F→R/__M and R→H/__M. Unfortunately, an appeal to contrast preservation will not work for Changting Hakka as it did for Taiwanese – Table 43(b) shows rampant neutralization in tonal collocations. The OCP is not likely to be the underlying cause for tone sandhi in Changting Hakka because, in general, identical adjacent tones do not trigger sandhi. NoCP might work for H+R/M→F+R/M, but that would not cover why F→L/__H. Many of these tone sandhi patterns can be articulated in the notation of tone feature operations (see Figure 21).

The list in Figure 21 is incomplete as there are some alternations that do not easily lend themselves to such a formulation, including /LH/→[MH], /FF/→[MF], and /FL/→[RF].

In addition to the difficulties outlined in the preceding paragraphs, the patterns of Changting Hakka tone sandhi put the spotlight on the issue of directionality, which is the theme of the ensuing section. While in Tianjin and Longyan, sandhi is consistently regressive (i.e., it is the first tone of a ditonal sequence that undergoes alternation), or consistently progressive in Hakha Lai (i.e., the second of a ditonal sequence undergoes alternation), Changting Hakka shows no such consistency. This will become more visually evident if Table 43(b) is presented in terms of SPE-type rules.

Regressive sandhi

$$\text{M, L} \rightarrow \begin{cases} \text{M} / \_ \text{ H, M, F} \\ \text{L} / \_ \text{ R, L} \end{cases}$$

$$\text{R} \quad \rightarrow \quad \text{H} / \_ \text{ M}$$

$$\text{H} \quad \rightarrow \quad \text{F} / \_ \text{ M, R, L}$$

$$\text{F} \quad \rightarrow \quad \begin{cases} \text{R} / \_ \text{ M} \\ \text{L} / \_ \text{ R, H} \\ \text{M} / \_ \text{ F} \end{cases}$$

Progressive sandhi

$$\text{L} \quad \rightarrow \quad \text{F} / \text{R} \_\_\_$$

Bidirectional sandhi

$$\text{FL} \quad \rightarrow \quad \text{RF}$$

Longyan Min and Changting Hakka are probably just two of many difficult cases. They may not be very well known because journals generally do not publish problems that have not been solved. By presenting them here, we hope that phonological theorizing might find inspiration in them as we become aware of how much more there is still to explore.

In this section, we tried to show tone sandhi to be a set of phenomena that may be triggered by different mechanisms. There is one other complication that must not be overlooked in understanding tone sandhi. Whatever the triggering mechanism, sandhi appears to apply in certain orders, as if there were a kind of 'directionality'.

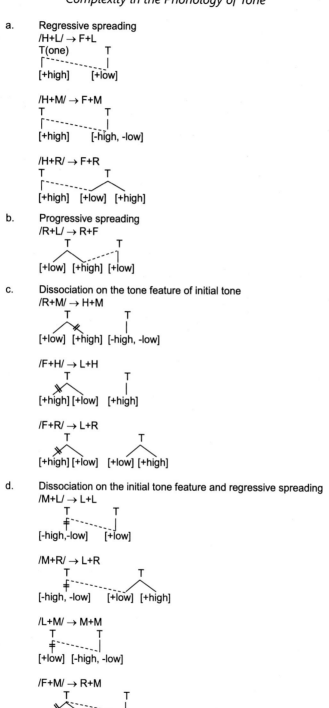

Figure 21 Changting Hakka tone sandhi in autosegmental notation
(adapted from Chen *et al.* 2004)

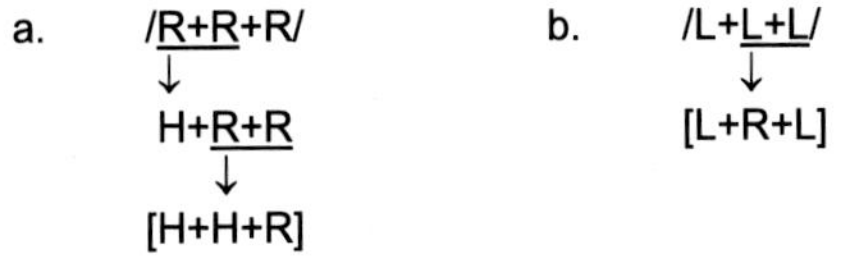

a.   /R+R+R/   b.   /L+L+L/
         ↓   ↓
      H+R+R   [L+R+L]
         ↓
      [H+H+R]

Figure 22 Directionality dilemma in Tianjin

6 Complexity in Directionality

Recall the ditonal sandhi patterns of Tianjin from Table 35. In all cases, it is the initial tone that undergoes sandhi. Imagine now a tritonal sequence, XYZ, such that XY and YZ are sandhi-tiggering sequences. If both X and Y alternated respectively to X' and Y', then sandhi must have applied first to the left window XY before applying to the right window YZ. If only Y→Y', then the right window is processed before the left, which bleeds XY sandhi from applying. Both turn out to be attested in Tianjin (see Figure 22).

Given an input sequence of three rising tones /RRR/ in Tianjin that is morphosyntactically flat (e.g., *jiu.wu.jiu* '9–5–9'), the output tone sequence is [HHR]. This result is obtainable by a self-counterbleeding ordering where the R→H/__R rule applies first to the left window before moving to the right, as illustrated in Figure 22(a). This left-to-right application, however, does not apply to /LLL/ inputs that are morphosyntactically flat (e.g., *ba. san.yi* "8–3–1"). In this case, the application is from right to left. With an inventory of four tones, there are sixty-four (=4^3) tritonal combinations. Given the six rudimentary ditonal sandhi rules, twenty-five of these sixty-four do not contain any sandhi sites (e.g., HHH, HLF, etc.), and twenty-four require only one adjustment (e.g., RRH→HRH, FLR→HLR, etc). The fifteen interesting cases that remain are shown in Table 44.

Contrary to Table 44's suggestion that Tianjin tone sandhi is oblivious to syntactic constituency, it is in fact always possible to apply tone sandhi starting from the minimum morphosyntactic constituent and terminating at any constituency boundary. In addition, this table does not present various optional outputs of tritonal sandhi. The interested reader is referred to Wee (2004: chapter 3) for discussion and to Wee, Yan and Chen (2005) for the complete fieldwork data. This table is kept uncluttered so that directionality issues are not obscured.

Along the 'input' column in Table 44, the first window of sandhi is indicated by underlining. For patterns P1–P14, the direction of sandhi application is important in arriving at the right output. Sandhi must apply from the left window to the right for P3, P4, P7, and P9. For P1, P2, P5, P6, P8, and P10–

Table 44 Directionality patterns in Tianjin tritonal sandhi (adapted from Wee 2004: 110)

Pattern	Input	Output	[x x] x	x [x x]	x x x
P1	LL<u>L</u>	LRL	[tuo.la] ji 'tractor'	kai [fei.ji] 'fly a plane'	san.san.san 'three three three'
P2	FF<u>F</u>	HLF via FLF	[su.liao] bu 'plastic cloth'	ya [re.dai] 'subtropical'	yi.da.li 'Italy'
P3	RR<u>R</u>	HHR via HRR	[li.fa] suo 'barber shop'	mu [lao.hu] 'tigress'	ma.zu.ka 'mazurka'
P4	<u>F</u>FL	LHL via LFL	[si.ji] qing 'evergreen'	zuo [dian.che] 'take a tram'	si.si.san 'four.four.three'
P5	L<u>F</u>F	RLF via LLF	[wen.du] ji 'thermometer'	tong[dian.hua] 'make a phone call'	san.si.si 'three four four'
P6	F<u>L</u>L	FRL	[lu.yin] ji 'tape recorder'	shang [fei.ji] 'board a plane'	si.san.san 'four three three'
P7	RR<u>H</u>	HLH via HRH	[xiao.pin] wen 'short prose'	xie [san.wen] 'write an essay'	jiu.wu.ling 'nine five zero'
P8	R<u>L</u>L	HRL via RRL	[bao.wen] bei 'thermos cup'	da [guan.qiang] 'speak in a bureaucratic tone'	ma.la.song 'marathon'
P9	RR<u>F</u>	HLF	[yang.lao] yuan	gui [ba.xi]	jiu.wu.si

Table 44 (cont.)

Pattern	Input	Output	[x x] x		x [x x]		x x x	
P10		via HRF		'old folk's home'		'pranks'		'nine five four'
	RFF	RLF	[gan.tan] ju		xie [bao.gao]	'write a report'	wu.si.si	'five four four'
P11	LRH	LLH	[xin.li] xue	'exclamation clause'	gao [shui.ping]	'high standard'	san.wu.ling	'three five zero'
				'psychology'				
P12	LRF	LLF	[zhong.biao] dian		xin [shou.tao]	'new gloves'	san.wu.si	'three five four'
				'timepiece store'				
P13	FRH	FLH	[jia.shi] yuan		po [jiu.ping]		si.jiu.ling	'four nine zero'
				'driver'		'broken wine bottle'		
P14	FRF	FLF	[dai.biao] hui		shang [li.bai]	'last week'	si.jiu.si	'four nine four'
				'representative meeting'				
P15	RFL	LHL	[bao.zheng] shu		xiao [jiao.che]		wu.si.san	'five four three'
				'guarantee certificate'		'small sedan car'		

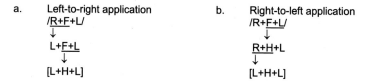

a.   Left-to-right application   b.   Right-to-left application

Figure 23 Indifference in direction of tone sandhi for Tianjin /RFL/ (cf. P15)

	Left-to-right		Right-to-left	
a. /L+L+L/ cf. P1	input:	/L+L+L/ ↓ R+L+L ↓	input:	/L+L+L/ ↓ L+R+L ↓
	output (i):	*[R+R+L] ↓ *backtracking* (ii): *[H+R+L]	output:	[L+R+L]
b. /F+F+F/ cf. P2	input:	/F+F+F/ ↓ L+F+F ↓	input:	/F+F+F/ ↓ F+L+F ↓
	output (i):	*[L+L+F] ↓ *backtracking* (ii): *[R+L+F]	output:	[H+L+F]
c. /R+R+R/ cf. P3	input:	/R+R+R/ ↓ H+R+R ↓	input:	/R+R+R/ ↓ R+H+R ↓
	output:	[H+H+R]	output:	*[L+H+R]

Figure 24 Establishing default directionality in Tianjin tritonal sandhi
(based on Chen 2000)

P14, the directionality is from right to left. Only P15 is indifferent to direction of sandhi application, as illustrated in Figure 23.

Chen's (2000: 105–49) original analysis discovered a number of priorities at work in the traffic of Tianjin sandhi, the first of which was that the default direction must have been left to right. The direction flips if the default operation ended with a sandhi-triggering sequence. The effect can be seen through Figure 24. The greyed-out cells are those for which the derivation is incorrect.

Let us start with Figure 24(a). Had sandhi windows moved left to right, /LLL/ would have produced [RRL], which contains a sandhi-triggering adjacency of Rs. This is not a well-formed output. To resolve that, the sandhi window must backtrack to produce [HRL]. In contrast, moving the sandhi window right to left produces [LRL] with no further sandhi-triggering collocations. Derivational economy and

	Left-to-right		Right-to-left	
a. /F+F+L/ cf. P4	input:	/F+F+L/ ↓ L+F+L ↓	input:	/F+F+L/ ↓
	output:	[L+H+L]	output:	*[F+H+L]
b. /F+L+L/ cf. P6	input:	/F+L+L/ ↓ H+F+L ↓	input:	/F+L+L/ ↓
	output:	*[H+R+L]	output:	[F+R+L]
c. /R+R+F/ cf. P9	input:	/R+R+F/ ↓ H+R+F ↓	input:	/R+R+F/ ↓
	output:	[H+L+F]	output:	*[R+L+F]
d. /R+F+F/ cf. P10	input:	/R+F+F/ ↓ L+F+F ↓	input:	/R+F+F/ ↓
	output:	*[L+L+F]	output:	[R+L+F]

Figure 25 Establishing priority of sandhi application in Tianjin
(based on Chen 2000)

well-formedness argue for a right-to-left directionality. The same is true for Figure 24(b). However, such an argument would erroneously lead us to choose a right-to-left directionality for /RRR/ (see Figure 24(c)). The solution must be that by default, the sandhi window moves left to right, thus /RRR/→HRR→HHR, even if it were not derivationally more economical than a leftward application. That default directionality is flipped when it fails to produce a well-formed sequence.

The second observation that Chen (2000) made was that sandhi rules applying to adjacency of identical tone contours (i.e., L+L, R+R, F+F types) must be resolved before those applying to adjacency of identical tone features (i.e., F+L, R+H, R+F types) (see Figure 25).

As may be seen in Figure 25, default directionality is not an issue here. In all cases, it is just that sandhi to LL, RR, and FF input sequences must apply first. Effects of directionality in the cases above are epiphenomenal.

Finally, evidence that backtracking is not allowed can be discerned through looking at cases of sandhi applying to adjacent tone features that are identical.

Figure 26 shows how in all cases, the default left-to-right direction would apply. Crucially, no backtracking can have been possible. Further, as mentioned earlier, sandhi applied to /LL/, /RR/, and /FF/, having taken precedence over sandhi to /FL/, /RH/, and /RF/, may not reapply even if the latter kind of sandhi produces adjacency of identical tone contours.

	Left-to-right	Right-to-left
a. /L+R+H/ cf. P11	input: /L+R+H/ ↓ L+R+H ↓ output: [L+L+H] ↓ *backtracking* *[R+L+H]	input: /L+R+H/ ↓ L+L+H ↓ output: *[R+L+H]
b. /L+R+F/ cf. P12	input: /L+R+F/ ↓ L+R+F ↓ output: [L+L+F] ↓ *backtracking* *[R+L+F]	input: /L+R+F/ ↓ R+L+F ↓ output: *[L+L+F]
c. /F+R+H/ cf. P13	input: /F+R+H/ ↓ F+R+H ↓ output: [F+L+H] ↓ *backtracking* *[H+L+H]	input: /F+R+H/ ↓ F+L+H ↓ output: *[H+L+H]
d. /F+R+F/ cf. P14	input: /F+R+F/ ↓ F+R+F ↓ output: [F+L+F] ↓ *backtracking* *[H+L+H]	input: /F+R+F/ ↓ F+L+F ↓ output: *[H+L+F]

Figure 26 Evidence against backtracking in Tianjin

Tianjin tritonal sequences show an intricate pattern of directionality because tone sandhi applied to ditonal sequences could create other sandhi-triggering environments. One can imagine the kinds of complexity that would arise in languages like Changting Hakka where rudimentary ditonal sandhi rules already involve both regressive and progressive patterns of alternation. The patterns are so complex that Chen *et al.* (2004) dedicated an entire monograph to explaining the data and patterns, but fell short of finding a coherent account.

Section 6 shows that sandhi rules can apply in certain orders that may best be characterized as directionality. The result of this is a combination of opaque and transparent rule-ordering that might not be said to be (counter-)feeding or (counter-) bleeding applying across the board. This remains a rich area for research, as patterns of many languages remain unaccounted for. Such patterns are most evident when tones concatenate into tritonal or longer strings. Tones, however, also interact with other phonological entities, which will be the subject of the next section.

7 Complexity in Interaction

Although there is plenty of evidence for tones existing on a separate dimension from the segments and syllables, there is also a lot of interaction between them (Haudricourt 1954, Kingston 2011, Gehrmann 2022). In Section 4.2, we already saw that codas have an effect on which tones are licensed, through examples such as Hausa, Navajo, and, in more detail, Thai. Similarly, in Section 3.1, we saw how voicing specifications of onset consonants relate to tone register in Songjiang. This section takes a deeper look at such interactions.

7.1 Influence from Coda Loss

In most theories of tonogenesis, languages evolve tone contours to preserve any contrasts that may result from the loss of coda consonants (see Hyslop (2009) for an excellent summary of such classics as Maspero (1912), Haudricourt (1954), Matisoff (1970, 1973, 1999), Mazaudon (1977), Hombert (1978), Thurgood (2002), and Gehrmann (2022) for an updated model and data with Austroasiatic languages). This theory is supported by the fact that languages with lexical tone contrasts tend to have very restricted codas. Maddieson (2013) surveyed 527 languages and found that if a language has complex tone contours, it is less likely to have complex syllable structures, even if that language might have a relatively large inventory of consonants and vowels.

A particularly telling case of how coda loss relates to the emergence of tone contours can be seen in the Kiranti language of Khaling. Khaling appears to have recently innovated a system of lexical tones, as can be seen through comparison of cognate items in its sister languages Limbu and Dumi (Jacques 2016).

Khaling has only two tones, high and falling, as may be seen in *mêm* 'he', *mêm* 'mother', *méê* 'there', and *mèê* 'rolling quickly'. In syllables with short vowels, this tone contrast is neutralized, that is, there is no falling or high tone contrast for *mɛ* 'that'. By comparison of cognate terms in sister languages, one can see that the falling tone in Khaling comes from two sources: the loss of the coda obstruent and the reduction of disyllables into monosyllables (see Table 45).

The Pre-Khaling forms, indicated with an asterisk *, may be constructed through a comparison of the cognate forms in Dumi, Limbu, and Khaling. Since both Limbu and Dumi have no contrast for tones, it is quite likely that Pre-Khaling did not have lexical tone either. From Table 45(a), it appears that the loss of the obstruent coda in Khaling is accompanied by the presence

Table 45 Emergence of tone contours in Khaling (Jacques 2016)

a. Falling tones from obstruent coda loss

Pre-Khaling	Limbu	Dumi	Khaling	
*bit	pit	bhiʔi	bâj	'cow'
*met	met	meeʔe	mêj	'wife'
*rak	yak		róò	'cliff'
*pak	phak	poʔo	póò	'pig'
*ʔik	ik		ʔúù	'field'

b. Falling tones from nasalization of obstruent codas

Pre-Khaling	Limbu	Dumi	Khaling	
*lop-na		lop-nɨ	lóò-nɛ	'to catch'
*rep-na	yɛps-	rep-nɨ	rêm-nɛ	'to stand'
*set-na	sɛt-	set-nɨ	sên-nɛ	'to kill'

c. Falling tones from reduction of disyllabic forms

Pre-Khaling	Dumi	Khaling	
*tsili	tsili	tsîl	'anger'
*meri	miri	mêr	'tail'
*noru	nurɨ	nôr	'tiger'
*nolu	nulɨ	nôl	'daytime'
*nam-ni	naamnɨ	nêm	'in two days'

of a falling tone contour (cf. Thai in Section 4.2). Dumi and Limbu retain the obstruents and neither of them has evolved lexical tone. Table 45(b) presents a similar case, only this time the presence of nasals must be responsible for the falling tone. Although not shown in the tables above, it should be noted that in cases where the Pre-Khaling form did not involve obstruent codas, modern Khaling cognates bear a level high tone. For example, Pre-Khaling *lam* 'road' and *k^hur* 'hand' are, in modern Khaling, lém and k^hár respectively. A viable theory that accounts for these facts must be one that attributes the genesis of tone contours to coda reduction. Finally, in Table 45(c), we see corroboration that the reduction of segmental complexity is a cause for tone contour in how disyllabic forms when reduced to monosyllables in Khaling is coincidental with the generation of the falling tone contour.

Table 46 Onset voicing and vowel's F0 peaks in English
(Lehiste and Peterson 1961, Lea 1973, cited in Peng 1992: 256)

	Lehiste and Peterson (1961) (Hz)	Lea (1973) (Hz)
m	162	165
n	161	156
l	164	160
r	166	160
j	164	161
b	165	162
d	163	151
p	175	170
t	176	172
ʃ	173	168

7.2 Influence from Onset Voicing

Unlike coda consonants, which impact on tone only through their loss and reduction, onset consonants interact with tone through their presence, even if their voicing is subsequently lost. Recall that in Songjiang the voicing of onsets remains contrastive in tandem with contrast in tone height. The voicing specifications of onsets have been known to phonetically affect the F0 of subsequent vocalic segments. In general, F0 peaks of the vowels following sonorant onsets are lower than the F0 peaks of vowels following voiceless obstruent onsets, as exemplified in English in Table 46.

English is not normally considered tonal even though F0 is an important cue for stress (Fry 1955, 1958). Table 46 is hence a tone-neutral example of F0 interaction with onset voicing. Until Maddieson's (1984) study on Burmese, it was thought that the F0-depressing effect of voiced consonants do not extend to sonorants. However, as Table 47 shows, sonorants participate in these effects as well. With Songling, one can see that aspiration may be a third option (Table 48).

The effect of voicing on tone is very widespread (see Peng (1992) for a comprehensive study), and has been viewed as the impetus of the creation of tone height or register differences in most theories of tonogenesis. A particularly corroborative case can be seen in Punjabi, where distinctions in the Voice Onset Time (VOT) contrast between aspirated voiced onsets and the unaspirated voiceless ones have recently collapsed. However, such syllables are prevented from neutralization through enhanced pitch differences (Kanwal and Ritchart 2015). Whether

Table 47 Means of F0 at vowel onset after sonorant consonants in Burmese
(Maddieson 1984)

	Falling (Hz)	Rising (Hz)	Creaky (Hz)
[-voice] = [m̥, n̥, ɲ̥, ŋ̥, l̥]	226	203	227
[+voice] = [m, n, ɲ, ŋ, l]	182	178	193
variation	44	25	34

Table 48 Tones in Songling (Chen 2000: 10)

Middle Chinese Tone Category	Onset obstruents	Voiceless	
	Plain	Aspirated	Voiced
Ping	[55]	[33]	[13]
Shang	[51]	[42]	[31]
Qu	[412]	[312]	[212]
Ru	[5]	[3]	[2]

Table 49 Ngizim tone–voice correlation (Peng 1992: 13–14)

a. Blocking H spread

voiced onset:	ná + dàwá-u	→ ná-dàwá-u	'I fed'
voiceless onset:	ná + tàan-u	→ ná-táàn-u	'I remembered'
sonorant onset:	ná + nùm-u	→ ná-nûm-u	'I constructed'

b. Blocking L spread

voiced onset:	à + dúb´s-í	→ à-dùb´s-í	'hide!'
voiceless onset:	à + tásh-í	→ à-tásh-í	'find!'
sonorant onset:	à + náng-í	→ à-nàng-í	'abuse!'

Punjabi will develop a more sophisticated tonal system of contours from this split of tone heights remains to be seen, although it is not likely within our lifetimes.

While the above issues appear to be largely phonetic, there are phonological processes that compel us to consider how these effects may be modelled in terms of tonal entities and phonological features. Ngizim (Table 49) and Nupe (Table 50) both show that the voicing specifications of consonants can block tone spreading.

Table 50 Low-tone spreading and blocking in Nupe
(Hyman 1970)

Infinitive	Progressive	Gloss
twá	è twá	'trim'
tyá	è tyá	'be mild'
bwá	è bwǎ	'be sour'
gbyá	è gbyǎ	'strip'

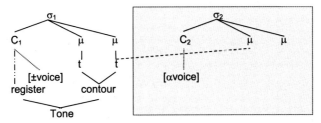

Figure 27 Voicing and tone in an autosegmental framework

In Ngizim, the tone of the prefix spreads to the first syllable of its stem. However, the high tone feature is blocked from spreading if the stem begins with a voiced consonant. In direct contrast, the low-tone feature would be blocked by a voiceless consonant. In Nupe, it is the low-tone feature that spreads from prefix to stem, which would be blocked by voiceless consonants.

Peng (1992) points out that such effects require a framework that addresses the crossing from the voicing of consonants to the tone features. For starters, one must allow for tone register to be read off the voicing specifications of onset consonants. Since it has been established that the mora is a TBU (recall Section 4), the handiest model might be along the lines of Figure 27.

In Figure 27, ignoring the grey box for the moment, Tone is envisaged as comprising of register and contour. Tone is mapped to the entities of a syllable through the terminal nodes, such that the tone features are associated with the moras, and the register with the pre-moraic consonant (i.e., C_1 in Figure 27). The voicing specifications of C_1 can be made to influence tone via some kind of constraint that requires concordance between [voice] and register. When the voicing contrast is lost, the [voice] feature can be said to be phonologically unspecified, and register is free to contrast. This takes care of cases like Songjiang and Punjabi, while allowing languages like Cantonese to have split registers even though obstruents have no voicing contrast anymore.

To get from Figure 27 to an account for Ngizim is much harder. It is not clear how the spreading of tone features can be blocked by the voicing specifications

Table 51 Tone–stress interaction in Ayutla Mixtec
(Pankratz and Pike 1967, de Lacy 2002)

a.	Stress leftmost H-toned syllable that is followed by L		
	H'HL	[lú'lúrà]	'he is small'
	LM'HL	[lùlu'úrà]	'he is not small'
b.	Otherwise, stress leftmost H-toned syllable		
	'HHH	['ʃínírá]	'he understands'
	ML'H	[kunù'rá]	'his tobacco'
c.	Otherwise, stress leftmost M-toned syllable that is followed by L		
	L'ML	[tì'katʃìʔ]	'whirlwind'
	M'ML	[la'ʃarà]	'his orange'
d.	Otherwise, stress leftmost syllable		
	'LLL	['ʃàtùì]	'my trousers'
	'MMM	['ʃiɲura]	'his pineapple'

of C_2. As tone and phonological features are autosegments, there is no violation of well-formedness in the crossing of lines. The only power [αvoice] may have is to place any received tone feature from σ_1 to within σ_2's preordained pitch range through concordance of [αvoice] and any register associated with σ_2. Assuming Ngizim to have [high] and [low] tone features, such a move would give rise to a three- or four-way contrast for tone height in Ngizim, contrary to fact. Riding on whatever might have constrained Ngizim's tone inventory to a two-way contrast for tone height, perhaps one may look for a solution through a different kind of concordance, this time between the tone feature that spreads into σ_2 with C_2's [αvoice]. Finding the right architecture that would accommodate tone and its interaction with [voice] remains an open question, and we look forward to the promises of future research.

7.3 Influence on Stress

Recall from Section 4.3 that lenition can come in the form of tonelessness accompanied by reduction in syllable length even if the number of segments remain unchanged. This was one of the arguments for mora as a TBU. Unsurprisingly, analysts have considered toneless syllables to be prosodically weak, and moved on to interpret them as corresponding to unstressed syllables. Ayutla Mixtec presents a different case of stress–tone interaction (Table 51).

In the Mixtec data above, H stands for high tone, M for mid, and L for low. Respectively, vowels are given an acute accent for H and a grave for L; M vowels are unaccented. In this language, stress prefers the syllable with the highest tone preceding a low tone, but otherwise aligns itself to the left edge as much as possible. Ayutla Mixtec is interesting because it presents a case par excellence for

Syllable
Phonological Word
Foot
Phonological Phrase
Tone
Register
Contour
t1
t2

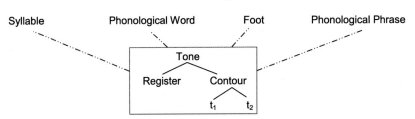

Figure 28 Tone associating with other domains

the co-existence of stress and tone in the same language. In many analyses of stress in tone languages, it is unclear whether such a postulation is necessary. For example, prosodic prominence in the first syllable of a Standard Chinese tone–toneless disyllabic string can be attributed to the presence of tone. In such cases, there is no need to make a claim for stress as a separate plane of prosody.

7.4 Interaction with Other Prosodic Domains

The preceding pages have treated tone largely as occurring within a syllable. This is explicitly encapsulated in Figure 27. However, given tone autosegmentality (cf. Section 4), one should expect tone to interface with larger domains. Figure 28 provides some logical possibilities.

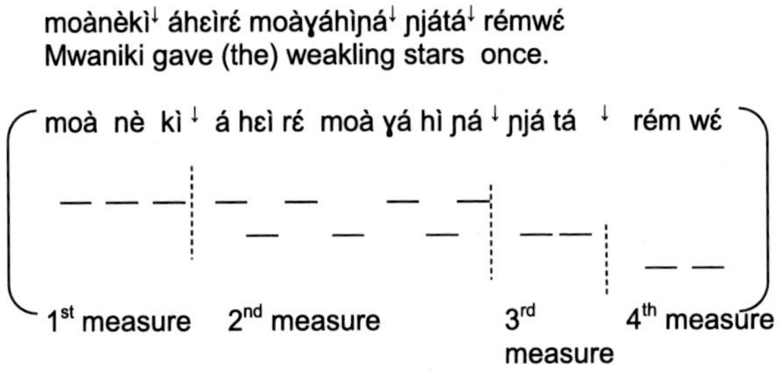

moànèkì↓ áhɛìrɛ́ moàɣáhìɲá↓ ɲjátá↓ rémwɛ́
Mwaniki gave (the) weakling stars once.
moà nè kì ↓ á hɛì rɛ́ moà ɣá hì ɲá ↓ ɲjá tá ↓ rém wɛ́
1st measure
2nd measure
3rd measure
4th measure

Figure 29 Tone terracing in Kikuyu (Clements 1983: 167, also Stewart 1993)

In the analysis of Ngizim in Section 7.2, we saw challenges that can come from working out how tone interfaces with syllables. These challenges were not evident if one were looking only at simple cases of tone spreading or at identifying the sites and targets of tone sandhi. For example, in Kera, tone is assigned to feet so that syllables in the same foot receive the same tone.

In Table 52, the foot structure in Kera is indicated with brackets, and ‘w’ and ‘s’ stand for weak and strong syllables respectively. Kera is iambic, with feet determined by vowel length, and they are therefore independent of tone assignment. As before, high tones are indicated with an acute accent á and low tones with a grave à, with mid tones here left unmarked. For ease of reference, the

Table 52 Tone patterns and foot structure in Kera trisyllabic words
(Pearce 2013: 141)

		(ws)s	(s)(ws)
/L/	LLL	(dìmìì)mì 'clothes'	(bɔ̀m)(bòrɔ̀ŋ) 'carp'
/H/	HHH	(kɘ́kám)ná 'chiefs'	(kúŋ)(kúrúŋ) 'skin bag'
/M/	MMM	(celɛɛ)rɛ 'commerce'	(kaŋ)(kɘlaŋ) 'hat'
/LH/	LLH	(gɘ̀dàà)mɔ́ 'horse'	unattested
	LHH	unattested	(dàk)(tɘ́láw) 'type of bird'
/HL/	HHL	(kɘ́sáá)bɔ̀ 'cricket'	unattested
	HLL	unattested	(mán)(dɘ̀hàŋ) 'bag'
/MH/	MMH	(tìlìŋ)kì 'hole'	unattested
	MHH	unattested	(taa)(mɔ́káá) 'sheep'
/HM/	HHM	(kú6úr)si 'burning coal'	unattested
	HMM	unattested	(sáá)(tɘraw) 'cat'

tonal sequence (H=high, M=mid, and L=low) of the syllables is also provided in the second column. The first column furnishes the basic tones involved.

It has been proposed in the literature that the same inventory of tones used for lexical contrasts can be extended to describe intonation patterns, for example using H and L autosegments for both tone and intonation (Pierrehumbert 1980, Ladd 2008) and notably in the Tones and Break Indices (ToBI) framework (see Truckenbrodt (2005) for ToBI analysis in German). That intonation might really just be phrase-level tone is reflected in Gussenhoven's (2012: 4) comment: 'analyzing the tonal system of a language without taking the intonation into account can be risky [since] … pitch phenomena may be assigned to lexical tones that belong to intonational tones'.

Tone's interface with large domains can be seen in tone terracing, illustrated in Figure 29 with Kikuyu.

Figure 29 shows a series of downsteps (the term was probably first used in Meeussen (1970: 270), see also Leben (2016)) over four measures. In the first measure, the three syllables carry the low tone. After downstepping into the second measure, the high tone of the later measure is only about as high as the low tone of the preceding one. This goes on iteratively. In languages exhibiting downstep such as Kikuyu, downstep is often triggered by the presence of a low tone, as exemplified in Dschang.

In Figure 30, the idea is that the deletion of *e* did not obliterate its associated low tone. That tone exerts its influence by lowering the following high tone in the form of a downstep. A demonstration of how that is done is neatly offered in Hyman's (1993) analysis using a model of tone, as given in Figure 31. At the risk

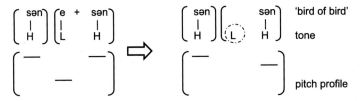

Figure 30 Downstep in Dschang (Pulleyblank 1983: 77)

μ   (TBU)
|
Tonal Root Node   (TRN = tone)
|
Tonal Node   (TN = tone contour)

Figure 31 Hyman's (1993) three-tiered model of tone

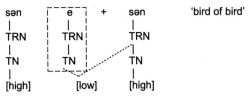

Figure 32 Downstep in Dschang using Hyman (1993)

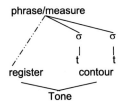

Figure 33 Terracing effect by register over a large domain

of conflating the intonational downstep of Kikuyu with vowel deletion downstep, Dschang may be accounted for as in Figure 32.

In Hyman's telling, the tone root node receives a low feature that depresses the interpretation of [high] under the tone contour. This is, in effect, treating the tone root node as register, cf. Figure 9(a). Figure 32, however, does not lend itself readily to capturing the long terraces of each measure in Kikuyu of Figure 29. To do so, one would need register to apply to a large domain of many syllables, akin to Figure 33.

In Figure 33, tone interfaces with some prosodic domain larger than the syllable. The register associates directly with the root node of the phrase/ measure while the contour features are shared across the syllables within that domain. Interaction between tone and register is probably more complex than this. In Hausa, for example, global raising of pitch range appears with 'yes-no' interrogative constructions, which appears to be a kind of intonational register.

Interestingly, that interacts with the lexical low tone as well (Inkelas, Leben, and Cobler 1986). This approach has the advantage of addressing a wide range of tonal phenomena using a single model of tone. However, it is speculative at this point, and much more research is needed on the exact implementation.

This section has presented a kind of miscellany on the phonological entities that tone can interact with. It draws upon evidence from both synchronic and diachronic accounts. In general, we find interaction with segments and with stress, as well as with different entities in morphosyntactic levels. The phenomena presented herein are not intended to be exhaustive, but as buoys seen from a wharf that signal the vast oceans ahead.

8 A Glimpse at Tone in the Arts

Given the role of lyrics and metre in the investigation of the syllable, and of intonation and pitch in the investigation of tone, we have included a discussion of the interaction between phonological tone and tone in other domains of artistic expression.

8.1 Phonology of Tone in Music

Given F0 as the fundamental property of tone, a natural question that arises is its relation with the melodic aspect of music (Schellenberg 2012, Ketkaew and Pittayaporn 2014, Ladd and Kirby 2020, Kirby 2021), bearing in mind that music is itself a complex entity that includes idioms, syntax, amusical noises, and rhythm among other things. Whether or not the pitch interval of tones in languages corresponds to some musical interval is a red herring. This is because musical intervals are dependent on the kinds of temperament one employs (e.g., just, harmonic, chromatic, . . .), and the allowances in variance for a match (recall Table 9). In this Element, we are also not concerned with whether a speaker of a tone language has a musical advantage or whether a musically trained child has a linguistic advantage. While this is a worthy area of research, it does not speak directly to the phonology of tone which is the theme of this essay. The critical issue for phonology is how tones remain discernible in singing, as musical melody and linguistic tone compete for the same F0 bandwidth. Logically, if linguistic tone is indomitable, then singing is speaking, and speakers of tone languages would never get to appreciate the aesthetic distinctions between the two. Conversely, if musical melody is free to override linguistic tone, then one would not expect any tonal unnaturalness between lyrics and tune. However, as churchgoers who attend Cantonese or Standard Chinese services would attest, traditional hymns translated into Chinese often render a rather sacrilegious ambiguity between 'Jesus the Lord' and 'Jesus the

a. Contour mirroring: the syllable's tone contour is mirrored in the musical tune
    e.g.

    [low]   [high]

    Syllable/Tone

b. Edge mirroring: intersyllabic tone features crossing is mirrored in the musical tune
    e.g.

    [high]   [low]

    Syllable/Tone-1 Syllable/Tone-2

c. Head faithfulness: intersyllabic tone head features' contrast is expressed in the
    musical tune
    e.g.

    [low] **[high]** [high] **[low]**

    Syllable/Tone-1   Syllable/Tone-2

Figure 34 Possibilities of tone-contrast preservation (Zhao 2020)

pig'. In many Chinese languages, the word for lord and master and the word for pig differ only in tone. Such translations, although grammatically and stylistically sound, simply do not work well in singing because of mismatch between tone and tune. In contrast, hymns composed in Chinese rarely have such awkwardness. Ergo, songs must somehow preserve linguistic tone contrasts. A few possibilities, as given in Figure 34, are worth considering.

Figure 34(a) is quite straightforward. The syllable has a rising tone, as indicated by the sequence of [low][high] features. The musical notes to which the syllable is attached ascend from G_3 to E_4. Such cases, where the music mirrors the tone contour, are a possibility for maintaining tone contrasts. Figure 34(b) is a case where the linguistic tone may not match neatly with the musical melody. Both syllables have flat tones, but are matched with rising musical melodies inconsistent with the tones' profiles. However, the second crotchet of Syllable/Tone-1 is higher than the first crotchet of Syllable/Tone-2. Such cases can be said to have mirrored the difference in tone height of the two syllables at the intersyllabic boundary, and can also be regarded as preservation of linguistic tone contrasts in the music. Figure 34(c) is more abstract. The syllables have contoured tones, rising and falling respectively. Of the two features that make up the contour tone, the second is the more important feature, that is, the head (indicated in boldface). The head contrast between the two syllables would be that Syllable/Tone-1 is [high] and Syllable/Tone-2 is [low]. This difference is preserved in the music because the third crotchet is lower than the second. At the transition between the two syllables, the musical pitch lowers, thus being faithful to the head tone feature.

Of the three possibilities, one may safely assume that satisfaction of Figure 34(a) would make for the easiest tone recognition in singing. Restricting themselves to only flat tones in Cantonese, Wong and Diehl (2002) showed that songwriters abandoned F0 ratio scale differences of read lexical tones and adopted an ordinal scale instead. This would suggest the possibility of Figure 34(b) at work. A deeper study might be required to see whether Figure 34(b) might be extended to include contour tones, but this seems to be feasible. If indeed so, that would argue for some form of edge effect of tones. Most phonologically interesting is Figure 34(c). If indeed the effects of headship of tone features within a tone contour are attested, that would add to a deeper understanding of phonological tone, as well as to the complexity of tone. Some evidence of this can be seen in the Beijing operatic arts. Yu (2008: 35, 87–95) reported the following observations.

Tone–tune correspondence in the Beijing operatic arts (Yu 2008: 35, 87–95)

a. T(one) 1 syllables should not be sung in notes **lower** than those of syllables with T2, T3, and T4.

b. T2 syllables should not be sung in notes **lower** than those of syllables with T1, T3, and T4.

c. T3 syllables should not be sung in notes **higher** than those of syllables with T1, T2, and T4.

d. T4 syllables should not be sung in notes **higher** than those of T1, T2, and T3.

e. Intonation profile and musical melody largely align. While there are counterexamples, musical devices (such as grace notes and melodic extensions) are often employed to mitigate misalignments.

    Beijing/Standard Chinese tones T1=[55], T2=[25], T3=[214, 21 or 35] depending on sandhi positions, T4=[51].

Yu's findings, which were largely based on studies carried out in the 1960s, were corroborated in Wee (2007), who studied folk songs sung in Standard Chinese. The results suggest that the tonal inventory is split so that T1 and T2 belong to one group and T3 and T4 in another. This is coincidental to the historical categories of Middle Chinese Ping and Ze (i.e., Shang, Qu and Ru, the non-Ping categories) also used in Tang metrical verse (more later in Section 8.2). However, modern songwriters are not likely to have strong intuitions about historical tone categories that preceded them by centuries, so it must be the case that there is something phonological underlying this split in modern Beijing/ Standard Chinese. Looking at effects on tone distortion under deliberate

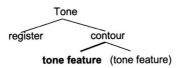

Figure 35 A tentative model of tone (cf. Figure 9(e))

lengthening of the spoken Standard Chinese tones, Wee argued that the split might be predicated on differences in the internal prominence of each tone.

Effects of lengthening (adapted from Wee 2007)
T1: *ma* [55] becomes [55555555]
T2: *ma* [25] becomes [23555555555], but *[222222235]
T3: *ma* [214] becomes [21111111114] or [21111111]
T4: *ma* [51] becomes [5311111111], but *[555555531]

From these observations, one can see that [high] is the feature that gets lengthened for T1 and T2, while [low] gets lengthened for T3 and T4. It is reasonable to postulate that even within the tone contour, there might be tonal headship of the constituent features. Yu's observations can be updated as: (i) T1 and T2 have the head feature [high], which should not be lower musically than adjacent syllables in singing; and (ii) T3 and T4 have the head feature [low], which should not be higher musically than adjacent syllables in singing. Tentatively accepting these ideas, the model of phonological tone may be updated as in Figure 35.

In most of the account given in this Element up to this point, a model like Figure 35 had been assumed. The update here is that one of the tone features is the head (boldface) while the other is a dependent. This raises other questions on the possibility of headship percolation akin to X-bar projection in syntax, but that has to be left open for future research.

8.2 Tone in Poetry

In metrical poetry, the usual understanding relates to a restriction in the number of lines or an organization of a number of syllables (varying between light and heavy) to form a line. In the former, common examples include ballads (thirteen lines), sonnets (fourteen lines), and the Malay pantun (two to sixteen lines in the form of couplets or quatrains). In organizing syllables, there are the French alexandrine (twelve syllables that may be organized into 2+4+2+4, 3+3+3+3 or 2+4+4+2 etc), the Japanese haikus (seventeen moras, typically broken into 5+7+5), and such feet as iambs, trochees, spondees, tribachs, dactyls, and bacchius, among others. Rarely does one find poetic metres that constrain tones such as that seen in the Chinese classical poetic forms such as the *jueju* (expandable to *lüshi* with two quatrains, or *pailü* with more) or *ci*. *Jueju* appeared around the Tang dynasty (618–927), while *ci* became popular in the Song dynasty (970–1127), and is believed to have evolved from earlier forms that relate to singing. In *ci* writing from the Song dynasty onwards, it is a matter of template filling – the template is presumably the skeletal remains of a song that has lost its musical score. An example is given using the example of 'Dielianhua'.

Ci **template for 'Dielianhua' ('Butterfly loves flowers')**
$[Z]Z[P]PPZZ_{rhyme}$。 $[Z]ZPP, [Z]ZPPZ_{rhyme}$。
$[Z]Z[P]PPZZ_{rhyme}, [P]P[Z]ZPPZ_{rhyme}$。
[repeat to make two stanzas]

In the template above, P stands for the Middle Chinese tone category *Ping*, and Z for all non-Ping tones, lumped together under the category *Ze*. Items in parentheses are default tone categories that may optionally be disobeyed. Rhyming syllables are indicated as Z_{rhyme}, which is interesting, as that indicates that rhyming requires tonal identity of some kind. This tonal requirement for rhyming is no longer enforced in modern Chinese song or poetry writing, a licence traditionally granted only to modern Chinese limericks and doggerel, even though its use in those genres is still prevalent as it is 'part of the fun'.

The main evidence that *ci* templates were derived from songs that have lost their music comes from the unevenness in the length of their lines. The term *ci* in modern Chinese also means song lyrics. If *ci* templates were indeed lyrical, then the Ps and Zs are probably requirements that aid discernment of tones in the musical melody (see Section 8.1). Specific to this particular example is that Ps and Zs are rarely isolated, and appear systematically and largely in pairs. This pairing pattern is strongest in the *jueju*, so that one is confronted with a clear case where tone seems to be used metrically (see Figure 36).

The schema shown in Figure 36 is for the heptasyllabic *jueju*. To get the pentasyllabic form, one needs only to remove the first two syllables, that is, (σ_1 σ_2). Incidentally, it is possible to reverse the Ps and the Zs to get a variant form. The

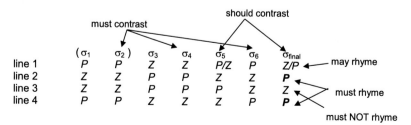

Figure 36 A schematic representation of a Tang verse stanza

main thing to see here is that, excepting σ_{final}, Ps and Zs occur in pairs. Note also that even-numbered syllables must contrast for tones, which leaves the odd-numbered ones some room for variation from the default. All these points suggest some kind of disyllabic iambic feet, defined by tone, are at work. The Tang dynasty ended more than a millennium ago, and it is hard to discern what the tonal properties were at that time in order to work out whether some kind of tonal headship or tonal complexity might underlie this poetic metre. It is also possible that tones might have accompanied syllable complexity or differences in syllable weight.

We do not know if tone interfaces only with music and poetry, but these are two obvious aspects, for which there is at least some evidence. In both cases, the interface appears to stem from either the melodic property of tone or the metrical use of tone. For the arts at least, we seem to find evidence for tone as input for the prosodic arts.

9 An Invitation

Tone is complex, even though in some languages it appears to be a simple contrast between high and low. In others, these can concatenate to produce contours, or even split into registers so that one is no longer sure whether the simple high-low contrast is a matter of register or of different points that might make a contour. Tones interact with one another to produce very intricate and complicated patterns. Sometimes it is possible to attribute these patterns to the avoidance of certain marked collocations, or to the preservation of contrast to avoid neutralization that has resulted from other changes. However, the triggers for tone sandhi in many other languages have remained elusive. Tonological research has come a long way since it first caught the attention of linguists, who tried to offer explanations for the dizzying array of patterns. Such explanations have come through postulating models of tone and through looking at how entities in these models interact with one another and with other linguistic entities. However, there is so much more that remains to be discovered and to be explained. Some of the challenging areas have been introduced in this Element, revealing quite unabashedly our inadequacies in explicating them. The phonology of tone is not something that we are ready at this time to offer a conclusion on. In lieu of that, and on behalf of the many scholars who have laboured to shed light on tone, we now extend a sincere invitation to you to join us.

References

Abramson, Arthur S. (1972). Tonal experiments with whispered Thai. In Albert Valdman (ed.), *Papers on Linguistics and Phonetics in Memory of Pierre Delattre*. The Hague: Mouton, pp. 31–44.

Akinlabi, Akinbiyi (1985). Tonal underspecification and Yoruba tone. PhD dissertation, University of Ibadan.

Akinlabi, Akinbiyi and Mark Liberman (2000). The tonal phonology of Yoruba clitics. In Birgit Gerlach and Janet Grijzenhout (eds.), *Clitics in Phonology, Morphonology and Syntax*. Amsterdam: John Benjamins, pp. 31–62.

Anderson, Doris (1962). *Conversational Ticuna*. Norman, OK: Summer Institute of Linguistics.

Anderson, Lambert (1959). Ticuna vowels; With special regard to the system of five tonemes. *Série Lingüistica Especial 1*. Rio de Janeiro: Publiçãos do Museu Nacional, pp. 76–119.

Andruski, Jean E. and Martha Ratliff (2000). Phonation types in production of phonological tone: The case of Green Mong. *Journal of the International Phonetic Association* 30: 37–61.

Asongwed, Tah and Larry M. Hyman (1977). Morphotonology of the Ngamambo noun. In Larry M. Hyman (ed.), *Studies in Bantu Tonology* (Southern California Occasional Papers in Linguistics 3). Los Angeles: University of Southern California, pp. 23–56.

Awobuluyi, Qladele (1978). *Essentials of Yoruba Grammar*. Oxford: Oxford University Press.

Banti, Giorgio (1988). Two Cushtic systems: Somali and Orono nounda. In Harry van der Hulst and Norval Smith (eds.), *Autosegmental Studies in Pitch Accent Systems*. Dordrecht: Foris, pp. 11–49.

Bao, Shijie (1998). *Hangzhouhua Cidian* [A dictionary of Hangzhou Chinese]. Nanjing: Jiangsu Education Publishing House.

Bao, Shijie (2003). *The Phonetic Database of Hangzhou*. Shanghai: Shanghai Education Press.

Bao, Zhiming (1990). On the nature of tone. PhD dissertation, Massachusetts Institute of Technology.

Bao, Zhiming (1999). *The Structure of Tone*. Oxford: Oxford University Press.

Barrie, Michael (2006). Tone circles and contrast preservation. *Linguistic Inquiry* 37.1: 131–41.

Bateman, Janet (1990). Iau segmental and tonal phonology. *Miscellaneous Studies of Indonesian and Other Languages* 10: 9–42.

Bearth, Thomas and Hugo Zemp (1967). The phonology of Dan (Santa). *Journal of African Languages* 6: 9–29.

Beckman, Mary E. (1986). *Stress and Non-stress Accent*. Dordrecht: Foris Publications.

Beijing [Beijing Daxue Zhongguo Yuyunwenxuexi Yuyanxue Jiaoyanshi] (ed.) (1989). *Hanyu Fangyin Zihui* [A collection of characters across Han dialects], 2nd edition. Beijing: Wenzi gaige chubanshe. (In Chinese.)

Bolinger, Dwight L. (1958). A theory of pitch accent in English. *Word* 14: 109–49.

Brunelle, Marc (2009). Tone perception in Northern and Southern Vietnamese. *Journal of Phonetics* 37: 79–96.

Brunelle, Marc and James Kirby (2016). Tone and phonation in Southeast Asian languages. *Language and Linguistics Compass* 10.4: 191–207.

Cai, Junming (1991). *Chaozhou Fangyan Cihui* [A dictionary of Chaozhou dialect]. Hong Kong: Institute of Chinese Culture, Chinese University of Hong Kong.

Chang, Charles B. and Yao Yao (2007). Tone production in whispered Mandarin. In Jürgen Trouvain (ed.), *Proceedings of the 16th International Congress of Phonetic Sciences*, August 6–10, Saarbrücken, Germany: University of SaarlandSaarbrücken, pp. 1085–88.

Chang, Kun (1953). On the tone system of the Miao-Yao Languages. *Language* 29: 374–8.

Chao, Yuen-Ren (1922). Zhonguo yuyan zidiao di shiyan yanjiu fa [Experimental methods in the study of Chinese language word tones]. *Kexue* [Science] vol. 7.9. (In Chinese). Reprinted in *Zhao Yuanren Yuyanxue Lunwenji* [A compilation of Chao's papers in linguistics]. Beijing: Commercial Press 2001, pp.27-36.

Chao, Yuen-Ren (1930). A system of tone letters. *La Maître Phonétique* 45: 24–7.

Chao, Yuen-Ren (1948). *Mandarin Primer*. Cambridge, MA: Harvard University Press.

Chao, Yuen-Ren (1968). *A Grammar of Spoken Chinese*. Berkeley: University of California Press.

Chen, Matthew Y. (2000). *Tone Sandhi: Patterns across Chinese Dialects*. Cambridge: Cambridge University Press.

Chen, Matthew Y., Lian-Hee Wee, and Xiuhong Yan (2008). The paradox of Hakka tone sandhi. In Yuchau E. Hsiao, Hui-chuan Hsu, Lian-Hee Wee, and Dah-an Ho (eds.), *Interfaces in Chinese Phonology*. Taipei: Institute of Linguistics, Academia Sinica, pp. 1–45.

Chen, Matthew, Xiuhong Yan, and Lian-Hee Wee (2004). *Hakka Tone Sandhi – Corpus and Analytical Challenges*. Journal of Chinese Linguistics Monograph Series No. 21. Berkeley: University of California. (In English and Chinese.)

Chuang, Ching-ting, Yueh-chin Chang, and Feng-fan Hsieh (2011). Productivity in Taiwanese tone sandhi *Redux*. In Wai Sum Lee and Eric Zee (eds.) *Proceedings of the 17th International Congress of Phonetic Sciences*. Hong Kong: International Phonetic Association, pp. 492–495. www.internationalphoneticas sociation.org/icphs-proceedings/ICPhS2011/OnlineProceedings/Regular Session/Chuang,%20Ching-ting/Chuang,%20Ching-ting.pdf.

Clements, G. Nick (1978). Tone and syntax in Ewe. In Donna Jo Napoli (ed.), *Elements of Tone, Stress and Intonation*. Washington, DC: Georgetown University Press, pp. 21–99.

Clements, G. Nick (1983). The hierarchical representation of tone features. In Ivan R. Dihoff (ed.), *Current Approaches to African Linguistics*, vol. 1. Dordrecht: Foris Publications, pp. 145–76.

Davison, Deborah S. (1982). Tianjin fangyan zhengzai jinxingde juanshe shengmude yanbiande fenxi [Analysis on the ongoing change of Tianjin retroflex onsets]. Paper presented at *the 15th International Conference on Sino-Tibetan Languages and Linguistics*. (In Chinese.)

de Lacy, Paul (2002). The interaction of tone and stress in Optimality Theory. *Phonology* 19.1: 1–32.

Dockum, Rikker (2018). Undocumented labor: How old fieldwork sheds new light on Tai tone system diversification. Presentation at *the 92nd Annual Meeting of the Linguistic Society of America*, 4–7 January 2018, Grand America, Salt Lake City. https://zenodo.org/record/1136317#.Y6LEJi0RpBx

Dockum, Rikker. (2019). The tonal comparative method: Tai tone in historical perspective. PhD dissertation, Yale University.

Edmondson, Jerold A. and Kenneth J. Gregerson (1992). On five-level tone systems. In Shina Ja J. Huang and William R. Merrifield (eds.), *Language in Context: Essays for Robert E. Longacre*. Arlington: Summer Institute of Linguistics and The University of Texas at Arlington, pp. 555–76.

Erickson, Donna M. (1976). A physiological analysis of the tones of Thai. PhD dissertation, The University of Connecticut.

Erickson, Donna, Kiyoshi Honda, Hiroyuki Hirai, and Mary E. Beckman (1995). The production of low tones in English intonation. *Journal of Phonetics* 23: 179–88.

Fry, Dennis B. (1955). Duration and intensity as physical correlates of linguistic stress. *The Journal of the Acoustic Society of America* 27: 765–8.

Fry, Dennis B. (1958). Experiments in the perception of stress. *Language and Speech* 1.2: 126–52.

Fu, Qian-Jie and Fan-Gang Zeng (2000). Identification of temporal envelope cues in Chinese tone recognition. *Asia Pacific Journal of Speech, Language and Hearing* 5: 45–57.

Gandour, Jackson (1974). On the representation of tone in Siamese. In Jimmy G. Harris and J. R. Chamberlain (eds.), *Studies in Tai Linguistics in Honor of William J. Gedney*. Bangkok: Central Institute of English Language, pp. 170–95. (Also published in *UCLA Working Papers in Phonetics* 27: 118–46.)

Gandour, Jackson (1977). On the interaction between tone and vowel length: Evidence from Thai dialects. *Phonetica* 34: 54–67.

Gao, Man (2002). Tones in whispered Chinese: Articulatory features and perceptual cues. MA thesis, University of Victoria.

Garellek, Marc, Patricia Keating, Christina M. Esposito, and Jody Kreiman (2013). Voice quality and tone identification in White Hmong. *Journal of the Acoustical Society of America* 133: 1078–89.

Gedney, William J. (1972). A checklist for determining tones in Tai dialects. In M. Estellie Smith (ed.), *Studies in Linguistics in Honor of George L. Trager*. The Hague: Mouton, pp, 423–37.

Gehrmann, Ryan (2022). Desegmentalization: Towards a common framework for the modeling of tonogenesis and registrogenesis in mainland Southeast Asia with case studies from Austroasiatic. PhD dissertation, The University of Edinburgh. DOI: http://dx.doi.org/10.7488/era/2364.

Gehrmann, Ryan and Rikker Dockum (2021). The East Asian voicing shift and its role in the origins of tone and register. Presented at *the 95th Annual Meeting of the Linguistic Society of America*, 7-10 January, Online.

Goldsmith, John A. (1976). Autosegmental phonology. PhD dissertation, Massachusetts Institute of Technology, published 1979 in New York: Garland.

Goldsmith, John A. (1978). English as a tone language. *Communication and Cognition* 11.3/4: 453–76.

Gordon, Matthew (2006). *Syllable Weight: Phonetics, Phonology, Typology*. New York: Routledge.

Guo, Chengming (1982). Tianjin fangyande zidiao xitong ji qi duiyu yingyu yudiao xuexide yingxiang [The impact of Tianjin tone system on learning English intonation]. MA thesis, Tianjin Normal University. (In Chinese.)

Gussenhoven, Carlos (2004). *The Phonology of Tone and Intonation*. Cambridge University Press.

Gussenhoven, Carlos. (2012). Tone and intonation in Cantonese English. In *Proceedings of the Third International Symposium on Tonal Aspects of Languages (TAL 2012)*, Nanjing, May 26-29, 2012. Paper ID O3-04. Accessed on 25 Dec 2014 from http://www.isca-speech.org/archive/tal_2012/tl12_O3-04.html.

Halle, Morris and Kenneth Stevens (1971). A note on laryngeal features. *MIT Research Laboratory of Electronics Quarterly Progress Report #101*.

Cambridge, MA: Massachusetts Institute of Technology, pp. 198–213. (Reprinted in Morris Halle (2003) *From Memory to Speech and Back: Papers on Phonetics and Phonology 1954–2002*. Berlin: Walter de Gruyter, pp. 45–61.)

Haudricourt, André-Georges (1954). De l'origine des tons en Viêtnamien [On the origin of tones in Vietnamese]. *Journal Asiatique* 242: 69–82.

Heeren, Willemijn F. L. (2015). Vocalic correlates of pitch in whispered versus normal speech. *The Journal of The Acoustical Society of America* 138.6: 3800–10.

Hoijer, Harry (1945). *Navaho Phonology*. Albuquerque: University of New Mexico Press.

Hollenbach, Barbara E. (1988). The asymmetrical distribution of tone in Copala Trique. In Harry van der Hulst and Norval Smith (eds.) *Autosegmental Studies on Pitch Accent*. Dordrecht: De Gruyter Mouton, pp. 167–82.

Hollenbach, Barbara E. (2008). *Gramática Popular del triqui de Copala*. Mexico City: Instituto Lingüístico de Verano, AC. [Electronic version]

Hombert, Jean-Marie (1978). Consonant types, vowel quality and tone. In Victoria Fromkin (ed.) *Tone: A Linguistic Survey*. New York: Academic Press, pp. 77–111.

Hsiao, Yuchau E. (2015). Tonal chain shifts in Taiwanese: A comparative markedness approach. In Yuchau E. Hsiao and Lian-Hee Wee (eds.), *Capturing Phonological Shades Within and Across Languages*. Newcastle upon Tyne: Cambridge Scholars Publishing, pp. 142–65.

Hsieh, Feng-fan (2008). Preservation of the marked as slope correspondence in Hangzhou Chinese. In Yuchau E. Hsiao, Hui-chuan Hsu, Lian-Hee Wee, and Dah-an Ho (eds.), *Interfaces in Chinese Phonology*. Taipei: Institute of Linguistics, Academia Sinica, pp. 223–42.

Hudak, Thomas J. (2008). *William J. Gedney's Comparative Tai Source Book*. *Oceanic Linguistics Special Publications* No. 34. Honolulu: University of Hawai'i Press.

Hudak, Thomas J. (2009). Thai. In Bernard Comrie (ed.), *The World's Major Languages*. London: Routledge, pp. 660–76.

Hyman, Larry M. (1970). How concrete is phonology. *Language* 46.1: 58–76.

Hyman, Larry M. (1978) Historical tonology. In Victoria A. Fromkin (ed.) *Tone: a Linguistic Survey*. New York: Academic Press. pp. 257–269.

Hyman, Larry M. (1981). Tone accent in Somali. *Studies in African Linguistics* 12: 169–203.

Hyman, Larry M. (1987). Prosodic domains in Kukuya. *Natural Language and Linguistic Theory* 5.3: 311–33.

Hyman, Larry M. (1993). Register tones and tonal geometry. In Keith Snider and Harry van der Hulst (eds.), *The Phonology of Tone: The Representation of Tonal Register*. New York: Mouton de Gruyter, pp. 75-108.

Hyman, Larry M. (2007) Universals of tone rules: 30 years later. In Tomas Raid and Carlos Gussenhoven (eds.) (2007) *Tones and Tunes*, Vol. 1: *Typological Studies in Word and Sentence Prosody*. Berlin: Mouton de Gruyter. pp.1-34.

Gussenhoven, Carlos (2012). Tone and intonation in Cantonese English. In *TAL-2012*, paper O3-04, accessed on 25 Dec 2014 from http://www.isca-speech.org/archive/tal_2012/tl12_O3-04.html.

Hyman, Larry M. and William R. Leben (2020). Tone systems. In Carlos Gussenhoven and Aoju Chen (eds.), *The Oxford Handbook of Language Prosody*, Oxford: Oxford University Press, pp. 45–65 (Unabridged manuscript version July 2017; https://escholarship.org/uc/item/97d2q41z.)

Hyman, Larry M. and Kenneth VanBik (2002) Output problems in Hakha Lai – or: What's (not) Chinese about directional tone sandhi. Keynote address given at *The Eighth International Symposium on Chinese Languages and Linguistics*, Academia Sinica, Taipei, 8-10 November 2002.

Hyman, Larry M. and Kenneth VanBik (2004). Direction rule application and output problems in Hakha Lai tone. *Language and Linguistics* 5.4: 821–61.

Hyslop, Gwendolyn (2009). Kurtöp tone: A tonogenetic case study. *Lingua* 119: 827–45.

Inkelas, Sharon, William R. Leben, and Mark Cobler (1986). The phonology of intonation in Hausa *North East Linguistics Society* 17.21. https://scholarworks.umass.edu/nels/vol17/iss1/21.

Jacques, Guillaume (2016). Tonogenesis and tonal alternations in Khaling. In Enrique L Palacar and Jean Leo Leonard (eds.) *Tone and Inflection: New Facts and New Perspectives*, pp. 41-66. Berlin: Mouton De Gruyter.

Kanwal, Jasmeen and Amanda Ritchart (2015). An experimental investigation of tonogenesis in Punjabi. In The Scottish Consortium for ICPhS 2015 (Ed.), *Proceedings of the 18th International Congress of Phonetic Sciences*. Glasgow, UK: the University of Glasgow. ISBN 978-0-85261-941-4. Paper number 0929 retrieved June 2016 from http://www.icphs2015.info/pdfs/Papers/ICPHS0929.pdf

Kenstowicz, Michael and Charles W. Kisseberth (1990). Chizigula tonology: The word and beyond. In Sharon Inkelas and Draga Zec (eds.), *The Phonology-Syntax Connection*. Chicago, IL: University of Chicago Press, pp. 163–94.

Ketkaew, Chawadon and Pittayawat Pittayaporn (2014). Mapping between lexical tones and musical notes in Thai pop songs. Presented at *the 28th*

Pacific Asia Conference on Language, Information and Computation (PACLIC 28), 12–14 December 2014.

Kingston, John (2011). Tonogenesis. In Marc van Oostendorp, Colin J. Ewen, Elizabeth V. Hume, and Keren Rice (eds.), *The Blackwell Companion to Phonology*. Wiley-Blackwell, pp. 2304–33.

Kirby, James (2021). Towards a comparative history of tonal text-setting practices in Southeast Asia. In Reinhard Strohm (ed.), *Transcultural Music History: Global Participation and Regional Diversity in the Modern Age.* Berlin: Berliner Wissenschafts-Verlag, pp. 291–312.

Kisseberth, Charles W. and Mohammad Imam Abasheikh (2011). Chimwiini phonological phrasing revisited. *Lingua* 121: 1987–2013.

Kuang, Jianjing (2013). The tonal space of contrastive five level tones. *Phonetica* 70: 1–23.

Kuo, Yu-Ching, Stuart Rosen, and Andrew Faulkner (2008). Acoustic cues to tonal contrasts in Mandarin: Implications for cochlear implants. *The Journal of the Acoustical Society of America* 123.5: 2815–24.

Kwan, Julia C. (1971). Ch'ing Chiang Miao phonology. *Tsing Hua Journal of Chinese Studies*. New series vol.9: 289–305.

Ladd, D. Robert. (2008). *Intonational Phonology.* Cambridge: Cambridge University Press.

Ladd, D. Robert and James Kirby (2020). Tone-melody matching in tone language singing. In Carlos Gussenhoven and Aoju Chen (eds.), *The Oxford Handbook of Language Prosody.* Oxford: Oxford University Press, pp. 676–87.

Ladefoged, Peter (1997). Instrumental techniques for linguistic phonetic field-work. In William Hardcastle and Joh Laver (eds.), *The Handbook of Phonetic Sciences.* Oxford: Blackwell Publishers, pp. 137–66.

Lea, Wayne A. (1973). Segmental and suprasegmental influences on fundamental frequency contours. In Larry Hyman (ed.), *Consonant and Tone: University of Southern California Occasional Papers in Linguistics* 1: 16–70.

Leben, William R. (1973). Suprasegmental phonology. PhD dissertation, Massachusetts Institute of Technology.

Leben, William R. (1978). The representation of tone. In Victoria Fromkin (ed.), *Tone: A Linguistic Survey.* New York: Academic Press, pp. 177–219.

Leben, William R. (2016). The nature(s) of downstep. Invited paper, *SLAO/1er Colloque International*, Humboldt Kolleg Abidjan 2014. In Firman Ahoua (ed.), *Challenges and New Prospects on Prosody in West Africa.* www.researchgate.net/publication/304784321_The_Natures_of_Downstep.

Leben, William R. (2017). Tone and length in Mende. In Margit Bowler, Philip T. Duncan, Travis Major, and Harold Torrence (eds) *Schuhschrift: Papers in*

Honor of Russell Schuh. Los Angeles: eScholarship Publishing, University of California, pp. 77-87. www.researchgate.net/publication/319873858_Tone_and_length_in_Mende

Lehiste, Ilsa and Gordon E. Peterson (1961). Some basic considerations in the analysis of intonation. *Journal of the Acoustical Society of America* 33: 419–25.

Li, Xingjian and Sixun Liu (1983). Tianjin fangyan cihui [Wordlist of the Tianjin dialect] *Hanyu Fangyanxuehui Dierjie Nianhui Lunwen* [The 2nd Annual Meeting of Society for Chinese Dialect Studies] (in Chinese).

Li, Xingjian and Sixun Liu (1985). Tianjin fangyan de liandu biandiao [Tone Sandhi in the Tianjin dialect]. *ZhongGuoYuWen*, vol.1985.1: 76–80. (In Chinese.)

Lin, Maocan and Jingzhu Yan (1980). Beijinghua qingsheng de shengxue xingzhi [Acoustic properties of tonelessness in Mandarin]. *Fangyan* [*Dialect*] 1980.3: 166–78. (In Chinese.)

Longacre, Robert E. (1952). Five phonemic pitch levels in Trique. *Acta Linguistica* 7: 62–8. DOI: https://doi.org/10.1080/03740463.1952.10415402.

Low, James (1828). *A Grammar of the Thai or Siamese Language*. Calcutta: The Baptist Mission Press.

Łubowicz, Anna (2003). Contrast preservation in phonological mapping. PhD dissertation, UMASS, Amherst, MA.

Łubowicz, Anna (2012). *The Phonology of Contrast*. Sheffield: Equinox.

Luo, Changpei (1956). *Hanyu Yinyunxue Daolun* [Introduction to Chinese Phonology]. Beijing: Zhonghua Shuju. (In Chinese.)

Ma, Qiuwu and Yuan Jia (2006). Two new third tone sandhi rules in Tianjin dialect: a critical reanalysis. *Journal of Tianjin Normal University* (Social science edition), 2006.1: 53–8. (In Chinese.)

Maddieson, Ian (1978). Universals of tone. In Joseph Greenberg (eds.), *Universals of Human Language, Volume 2: Phonology*. Stanford, CA: Stanford University Press, pp. 335–66.

Maddieson, Ian (1984). The effects of F0 of a voicing distinction in sonorants and their implications for a theory of tonogenesis. *Journal of Phonetics* 12: 9–15.

Maddieson, Ian (2013). Tone. In Matthew S. Dryer and Martin Haspelmath (eds.), *The World Atlas of Language Structures Online*. Leipzig: Max Planck Institute for Evolutionary Anthropology. http://wals.info/chapter/13.

Maspero, Henri (1912). Études sur la phone´tique historique de la langue Annamite: les initiales. *Bulletin de l'Ecole Francaise d'Extreme Orient* 12:1–126.

Matisoff, James A. (1970). Glottal dissimilation and the Lahu high-rising tone: a tonogenetic study. *Journal of the American Oriental Society* 90.1: 13–44.

Matisoff, James A. (1973). Tonogenesis in Southeast Asia. In Larry Hyman (ed.), *Consonant Types and Tone*. Los Angeles: Linguistics Program, University of Southern California, pp. 71–95.

Matisoff, James A. (1999). Tibeto-Burman tonology in an areal context. In Kaji Shigeki (ed.), *Proceedings of the Symposium 'Cross-Linguistic Studies of Tonal Phenomena: Tonogenesis, Typology, and Related Topics'*. Tokyo: Institute for the Study of Languages and Cultures of Asia and Africa, Tokyo University of Foreign Studies, pp. 3–32.

Matsukawa, Kosuke (2012). Phonetics and phonology of Chicahuaxtla Triqui tones. PhD dissertation, The University at Albany, State University of New York. https://search.proquest.com/docview/1032540083.

Mazaudon, Martine (1977). Tibeto-Burman tonogenetics. *Linguistics of the Tibeto-Burman Area* 3.2: 1–123.

McCawley, James (1978). What is tone? In Victoria Fromkin (ed.), *Tone: A Linguistic Survey*. New York: Academic Press, pp. 113–32.

Meeussen, Achille E. (1970). Tone typologies for West African languages. *African Language Studies* 11: 266–71.

Morén, Bruce and Elizabeth Zsiga (2006). The lexical and post-lexical phonology of Thai tones. *Natural Language and Linguistic Theory* 24: 113–78.

Nguyen, van Loi and Jerold Edmondson (1997). Thanh dieu va chat giong trong tieng Viet hien dai [The tones and voice quality in modern Northern Vietnamese: instrumental case studies]. *Ngon Ngu* 1:1–16.

Niimi, Seiji, Satoshi Horiguchi, and Noriko Kobayashi (1991). F0 raising role of the sternothyroid muscle – an Electromyographic study of two tenors. In Jan Gauffin and Britta Hammarberg (eds.), *Vocal Fold Physiology: Acoustic, Perceptual, and Physiological Aspects of Voice Mechanisms*. San Diego, CA: Singular Publishing Group, pp. 183–8.

Odden, David (1995). Tone: African languages. In John Goldsmith (ed.), *The Handbook of Phonological Theory*. Oxford: Blackwell Publishers, pp. 444–75.

Ohala, John J. (1972) How is pitch lowered? *Journal of the Acoustical Society of America* vol.52: 124.(A).

Ohala, John J. (1978). Production of tone. In Victoria A. Fromkin (ed.), *Tone: A Linguistic Survey*. New York: Academic Press, pp. 5–39.

Ohala, John J. and Hajime Hirose (1970). The function of the sternohyoid muscle in speech. *Annual Bulletin* 4: 41–4.)

Pallegoix, Jean-Baptiste (1854). *Description of the Thai Kingdom or Siam*. Paris: Mission de Siam.

Pankratz, Leo and Eunice V. Pike (1967). Phonology and morphotonemics of Ayutla Mixtec. *International Journal of American Linguistics* 33: 287–99.

Paulian, Christian (1974). *Le Kukuya: Langue Teke du Congo*. Paris: SELAF.

Pearce, Mary, D (2013) *The Interaction of Tone with Voicing and Foot Structure*. Stanford: CSLI Publications.

Peng, Long (1992). A unified theory of tone-voice. PhD dissertation, University of Arizona.

Peng, Long (2013). *Analyzing Sound Patterns: An Introduction to Phonology*. Cambridge: Cambridge University Press.

Perkins, Jeremy (2013). Consonant-tone tnteraction in Thai. PhD. dissertation, Rutgers University.

Pham, Andrea Hoa (2003). *Vietnamese Tone: A New Analysis*. New York: Routledge.

Pierrehumbert, Janet B. (1980) *The phonology and phonetics of English intonation*. PhD dissertation, MIT.

Pittayaporn, Pittayawat (2009). The phonology of Proto-Tai. PhD dissertation, Cornell University.

Prince, Alan and Paul Smolensky (1993/2004). *Optimality Theory: Constraint Interaction in Generative Grammar*. Malden, MA: Blackwell Publishing.

Pulleyblank, Douglas (1983). Tone in lexical phonology. PhD dissertation, Massachusetts Institute of Technology. (Published 1986, Dordrecht: D. Reidel.)

Qian, Nairong (1992). *Dangdai Wuyu Yanjiu* [Studies of contemporary Wu Chinese]. Shanghai: Shanghai Education Publishing House.

Rensch, Calvin R. (1968) *Proto-Chinantec Phonology*. Mexico City: Museo Nacional de Anthropologia.

Sarawit, Mary (1973). The proto-Tai vowel system. PhD dissertation, University of Michigan, Ann Arbor.

Sarawit, Mary (1975). Some changes in the final component of the Tai syllable. In J. G. Harris and J. R. Chamberlain (ed.), *Studies in Tai Linguistics in Honor of William J. Gedney*. Bangkok: Central Institute of English Language, Office of State Universities, pp. 316–28.

Schellenberg, Murray (2012). Does language determine music in tone languages? *Ethnomusicology* 56.2: 266–78.

Shi, Feng (1987). Tianjin fangyan danziyin shengdiao fenxi [Analysis of monosyllabic word tones in the Tianjin dialect]. *Yuyan Yanjiu Luncong* 4. (Reprinted in Feng Shi (ed.), *Studies in Tone and Stops*. Beijing: Beijing University Press, pp. 53-65, in Chinese.)

Shi, Feng, Lin Shi, and Rongrong Liao (1987). An experimental analysis of the five level tones of the Gaoba Dong language. *Journal of Chinese Linguistics* 15.2: 335–61.

Shih, Chi-lin (1986). The prosodic domain of tone Sandhi in Chinese. PhD dissertation, San Diego: University of California.

Shimizu, Kiyoshi (1971). Comparative Jukunoid: An introductory survey. PhD dissertation, University of Ibadan.

Sietsema, Brian M. (1989). Metrical dependencies on tone assignment. PhD dissertation, Massachusetts Institute of Technology.

Simmons, Richard VanNess (1992). The Hangzhou dialect. PhD dissertation, University of Washington.

Stewart, John M. (1993). Dschang and Ebrié as Akan-type total downstep languages. In Keith Snider and van Harry der Hulst (eds.), *The Phonology of Tone: The Representation of Tonal Register.* Berlin: Mouton de Gruyter, pp. 185–244.

Suárez, Jorge A. (1983) *The Mesoamerican Indian Languages.* Cambridge: Cambridge University Press.

Thomas, Guillaume (2008). An analysis of Xiamen tone circle. In Natasha Abner and Jason Bishop (eds.), *Proceedings of the 27th West Coast Conference on Formal Linguistics,* Somerville, MA: Cascadilla Proceedings Project, pp. 422–30.

Thurgood, Graham (2002). Vietnamese tonogenesis: Revising the model and the analysis. *Diachronica* 19.2, 333–63.

Thurgood, Graham (2007). Tonogenesis revisited: Revising the model and the analysis. In Jimmy G. Harris, Somsonge Burusphat, and James E. Harris (eds.), *Studies in Tai and Southeast Asian Linguistics.* Bangkok: Ek Phim Thai Ltd. pp. 263–91.

Truckenbrodt, Hubert (2005). A short report on intonation phrase boundaries in German. *Linguistische Berichte* 203: 273–96.

Voegelin, C. F. and Florence M. Voegelin (1965). Languages of the world: Sino-Tibetan Fascicle Three. *Anthropological Linguistics* 7.4: 1–77. http://files.eric.ed.gov/fulltext/ED010359.pdf.

Wall, Leon and William Morgan (1958). *Navajo–English Dictionary.* Window Rock, AZ: Navajo Agency, Branch of Education.

Wang, Feng (2012). *Yuyan Jiechu yu Yuyan Bijiao – yi Baiyu wei Li* [Language contact and comparison: the case of Bai]. Beijing: Commercial Press. (In Chinese.)

Wang, Jialing (2002). Sanzhong fangyan qingsheng de youxuanlun fenxi [An optimality theoretic analysis of three dialects]. *Linguistic Sciences* 2002.1: 78–85. (In Chinese.)

Wang, William S.-Y. (1967). Phonological features of tone. *International Journal of American Linguistics* 33.2: 93–105.

Wee, Lian-Hee (2004). Inter-tier correspondence theory. PhD dissertation, Rutgers University, NJ.

Wee, Lian-Hee (2007). Unraveling the relation between Mandarin tones and musical melody. *Journal of Chinese Linguistics* 35.1: 128–44.

Wee, Lian-Hee (2015). Prominence from complexity: Capturing the Tianjin ditonal patterns. *Language and Linguistics*, special issue on Theoretical Aspects of Chinese Phonology 16.6: 891–926.

Wee, Lian-Hee (2016a). Tone assignment in Hong Kong English. *Language: Phonological Analysis* 92.2: e112–32.

Wee, Lian-Hee (2016b). Hearing the inner voices of Asian English poets. Keynote paper presented at *The 5th International Conference for Language, Literature and Linguistics*, 30 May 2016, Singapore. www.researchgate.net/publication/303722160_Hearing_the_Inner_Voices_of_Asian_English_Poets.

Wee, Lian-Hee (2017). Tone, music and singing. In Rint Sybesma, Wolfgang Behr, Zev Handel, James. C. T. Huang, and James Myers (eds.), *Encyclopedia of Chinese Language and Linguistics*, vol. 4. Leiden: Brill, pp. 355–60.

Wee, Lian-Hee (2019). *Phonological Tone*. Cambridge University Press.

Wee, Lian-Hee (2020). A spin to preserve contrast: Taiwanese tone sandhi. In Seunghun Lee and Will Bennet (guest eds.), *Stellenbosch Papers in Linguistics Plus* (Special issue) 60: 13–29. DOI: https://doi.org/10.5842/60-0-755.

Wee, Lian-Hee, Xiuhong Yan, and Matthew Chen (2005). *Yinan yu Luxiang: Lun Tianjin Fangyan de Liandu Biandiao* [Conundrums and Directions: on Tone Sandhi in the Tianjin Dialect]. Beijing: Beijing Commercial Press. (In Chinese.)

Wei, Yuqing (2001). Neutral tone in Urumqi Chinese dialect: phonetic description and phonological analysis. Master's thesis, Tianjin Normal University.

Welmers, William E. (1973). *African Language Structures*. Berkeley : University of California Press.

Wong, Patrick C. M. and Randy L. Diehl (2002). How can the lyrics of a song in a tone language be understood? *Psychology of Music* 30.2: 202–9.

Woo, Nancy H. (1969). Prosody and Phonology. (PhD dissertation, Massachusetts Institute of Technology.)

Xu, Yi (2013). ProsodyPro – a tool for large-scale systematic prosody analysis. In *Proceedings of Tools and Resources for the Analysis of Speech Prosody* (TRASP 2013), August 30, 2013, Aix-en-Provence: Laboratoire Parole et Langage (LPL), pp. 7–10. Version 5.5.2. www.homepages.ucl.ac.uk/~uclyyix/ProsodyPro/.

Xu, Yue (2007). Hangzhou fangyande neibu chayi [Internal variations of the Hangzhou dialect]. *Fangyan* [Dialects] 2007.1: 10–14 (In Chinese.)

Yan, Hanbo and Jie Zhang (2016). Pattern substitution in Wuxi tone sandhi and its implication for phonological learning. *International Journal of Chinese Linguistics* 3.1: 1–44.

Yan, Xiuhong and Chao Luo (2008). Longyan (yanshi) hua de liandu biandiao [Tone sandhi in Longyan (Yanshi) Dialect]. Paper presented at *the 10th International Min Dialect Conference*, Zhanjiang Normal University.

Yip, Moira (1980). The tonal phonology of Chinese. PhD dissertation, Massachusetts Institute of Technology, Cambridge, Massachusetts. Published 1991, New York: Garland Publishing.

Yip, Moira (1989). Contour tones. *Phonology* 6: 149–74.

Yip, Moira (1995). Tone in East Asian languages. In John Goldsmith (ed.), *The Handbook of Phonological Theory*. Oxford: Blackwell Publishers, pp. 476–94.

Yip, Moira (2002). *Tone*. Cambridge: Cambridge University Press.

Young, Robert W. and William Morgan Sr. (1987). *The Navajo Language: A Grammar and Colloquial Dictionary*, revised edition. Albuquerque: University of New Mexico Press.

Yu, Huiyong (2008). *Qiangci Guanxi Yanjiu* [A study of the relation between lyrics and music]. Beijing: Zhongyang Yinyue Xueyuan Chubanshe. (In Chinese.)

Yun, Weili (1987). *Hainan Fangyan* [Hainan dialect]. Macau: University of Macau Press.

Zec, Draga (2011) Quantity-sensitivity. In Marc Van Oostendorp, Colin J. Ewen, Elizabeth Hume, and Keren Rice (eds.), *Blackwell Companion to Phonology*. Oxford: Wiley-Blackwell, pp. 1335–61.

Zhang, Jie (2002). *The Effects of Duration and Sonority on Contour Tone Distribution: A Typological Survey and Formal Analysis*. New York: Routledge.

Zhang, Jie (2014). Tones, tonal phonology, and tone sandhi. In C.-T. James Huang, Y.-H. Audrey Li, and Andrew Simpson (eds.), *The Handbook of Chinese Linguistics*. Oxford: Wiley-Blackwell, pp. 443–64.

Zhang, Jie and Yuwen Lai (2008). Phonological knowledge beyond the lexicon in Taiwanese reduplication. In Yuchau E. Hsiao, Hui-chuan Hsu, Lian-Hee Wee, and Dah-an Ho (eds.) *Interfaces in Chinese Phonology*. Taipei: Institute of Linguistics, Academia Sinica, pp. 183–222.

Zhang, Jie, Yuwen Lai, and Craig Sailor (2011). Modeling Taiwanese speakers' knowledge of tone sandhi in reduplication. *Lingua* 121.2: 181–206.

Zhang, Jie and Jiang Liu (2011). Tone sandhi and tonal coarticulation in Tianjin Chinese. *Phonetica* 68.3: 161–91.

Zhang, Jie and Jiang Liu (2016). The productivity of variable disyllabic tone sandhi in Tianjin Chinese. *Journal of East Asian Linguistics* (Appendix 1, Appendix 2, Appendix 3) 25.1: 1–35.

Zhao, Kaixin (2020). The role of melisma in language-music interface in Zuoquan folk songs. Master's thesis, Hong Kong Baptist University.

Acknowledgements

The authors owe thanks to the reviewers for their careful commenting. We are also grateful to the subjects, who must remain anonymous, and who participated in our experiments at the HKBU Phonology Lab; to Winnie H. Y. Cheung for her artwork with some of the diagrams and the various GIF files that enliven this Element; and to Feng-fan Hsieh for permission to reproduce his graph (Figure 7). This work is partially supported by Hong Kong Baptist University's Faculty Research Grant (FRG) Category II (Grant No. FRG2/17–18/076) and Hong Kong Government's Research Matching Grant Scheme (RMGS) (Project No. RMGS2019_1_18).

Cambridge Elements ≡

Phonology

Robert Kennedy

University of California, Santa Barbara

Robert Kennedy is a Senior Lecturer in Linguistics at the University of California, Santa Barbara. His research has focused on segmental and rhythmic alternations in reduplicative phonology, with an emphasis on interactions among stress patterns, morphological structure, and allomorphic phenomena, and socio-phonological variation within and across the vowel systems of varieties of English. His work has appeared in *Linguistic Inquiry, Phonology,* and *American Speech.* He is also the author of *Phonology: A Coursebook* (Cambridge University Press), an introductory textbook for students of phonology.

Patrycja Strycharczuk

University of Manchester

Patrycja Strycharczuk is a Senior Lecturer in Linguistics and Quantitative Methods at the University of Manchester. Her research programme is centered on exploring the sound structure of language by using instrumental articulatory data. Her major research projects to date have examined the relationship between phonology and phonetics in the context of laryngeal processes, the morphology-phonetics interactions, and articulatory dynamics as a factor in sound change. The results of these investigations have appeared in journals such as *Journal of Phonetics, Laboratory Phonology,* and *Journal of the Acoustical Society of America.* She has received funding from the British Academy and the Arts and Humanities Research Council.

About the Series

Cambridge Elements in Phonology is an innovative series that presents the growth and trajectory of phonology and its advancements in theory and methods, through an exploration of a wide range of topics, including classical problems in phonology, typological and aerial phenomena, and interfaces and extensions of phonology to neighbouring disciplines.

Cambridge Elements ≡

Phonology

Printed in the United States
by Baker & Taylor Publisher Services